THE WORLD WE HAVE

Also by Thich Nhat Hanh in Aleph

Touching Peace: Practising the Art of Mindful Living
Fidelity: How to Create a Loving Relationship That Lasts
Answers from the Heart: Practical Responses to Life's Burning Questions
How to Fight
No Mud, No Lotus: The Art of Transforming Suffering
Work: How to Find Joy and Meaning in Each Hour of the Day

THE WORLD WE HAVE

A BUDDHIST APPROACH TO PEACE AND ECOLOGY

THICH NHAT HANH

INTRODUCTION BY
ALAN WEISMAN

ALEPH

ALEPH

ALEPH BOOK COMPANY
An independent publishing firm
promoted by ***Rupa Publications India***

First published by Parallax Press in 2008

Published in India in 2023
by Aleph Book Company
7/16 Ansari Road, Daryaganj
New Delhi 110 002

Cover illustration by fayfena/Alamy Stock Photo

ISBN: 978-93-95853-16-3

1 3 5 7 9 10 8 6 4 2

For sale in India only.

Printed in India.

Every one of us can do something to protect and care for our planet. We have to live in such a way that a future will be possible for our children and our grandchildren. Our own life has to be our message.

—Thich Nhat Hanh

CONTENTS

FOREWORD

Many years ago, after burning out from political activism, in my search for a spiritual teacher who could guide me on how to 'be peace' rather than 'fight for peace', I arrived at a retreat for artists at the Ojai Foundation in California. In the five days that Thich Nhat Hanh taught there, I felt for the first time that rather than merely having a concept or notion of peace, I truly *experienced* peace. Each day we walked in meditative awareness among the sage bushes in the foothills of the Los Padres mountain, ate meals in silence, contemplated existential questions, and learnt how to live happily in the present moment.

Thay (as he is known to his students—it is pronounced like the first half of 'Thailand') taught by his example, his metaphors, and his practical, poetic, philosophical words. He taught us to cultivate the energy of mindfulness which would allow us, even in the most mundane of activities, to touch the miracle of life in the present moment.

When I returned home, I wrote him a letter to say that if he was interested in visiting India I would be happy to arrange something for him. As it happened, he had been planning to make a pilgrimage, 'In the Footsteps of the Buddha', and he requested me to organize this journey. It was in those thirty-five days of travel in close proximity that I came to see that I had found my spiritual guide, someone who blended everyday activities with a spiritual significance, someone who epitomized 'Engaged Buddhism'. His insights allowed me to link my inner practice to my outer social, political, and ecological concerns. As I discovered, I was not the only one whom he had affected in this way.

Thay had been instrumental in influencing Martin Luther King Jr. to come out against the war in Vietnam (which is Thay's homeland); in fact, King nominated him for the Nobel Peace prize in 1967, a year when it was not conferred on anyone. His Holiness the Dalai Lama said about Thay that 'he shows us the connection between a person's inner peace and peace on earth'. He has been revolutionary, being one of the first monks in Vietnam to ride a bicycle, to change the language of liturgy from classical Chinese to Vietnamese, to bring much greater gender equity in the Buddhist sangha (community), and even to introduce practices such as hugging meditation in order to make the Dharma more accessible to Americans. Unique in many ways, Thich Nhat Hanh was once described by another Zen master, Richard Baker Roshi, as a cross between a cloud, a snail, and a piece of heavy machinery.

On the actual path of the Buddha, Thay allowed me to understand the Buddha as a human being: one who had struggled with the existential questions of his time and discovered a path of awakening. Thay suggested that I continue this practice of pilgrimage that the Buddha had suggested; it would help me understand the Buddha and his teachings better. Each winter since 1988, I have gone on pilgrimage along the path of the Buddha, and at some time during each year I have gone on retreat with Thich Nhat Hanh.

As I got to know the Buddha better, he struck me as having been a practical man, whose core teachings were ways to overcome suffering and attain happiness, peace, and liberation. His concerns were rooted in our human experience, and not in metaphysical speculations on the existence of God or questions about eternity.

His discovery of the non-self and the interdependent nature of reality—for which Thich Nhat Hanh coined the word 'interbeing'—and his teaching that this understanding can be gained by one's own effort through the practices of mindfulness, concentration, and insight were revolutionary at the time. They continue to be counter-intuitive in a world where so much emphasis is placed on individuality and the self.

Thich Nhat Hanh has taken the ancient teachings of the Buddha, developed in India 2,600 years ago, and made them relevant to our time. The perennial questions of what binds us to suffering and what can give us a sense of inner freedom and awakening remain; but the means of practice have been skilfully adapted. Thich Nhat Hanh has taken many of the practices out of the monastaries and secularized them for an everyday audience. His school of Zen Buddhism, rooted in the 'Mind Only' (Vijñānavāda) School of Mahayana Buddhism, speaks about 'Store Consciousness' which holds many seeds, both wholesome and unwholesome. The basis of Thay's practice is to water the seeds of mindfulness, thereby becoming aware of our mental formations as they arise. In this way we become aware of the roots of those mental states and, in an internal weeding of our mind's garden, we cull or transform the unwholesome seeds and cultivate or quicken the wholesome ones.

Thay has made the Buddha Dharma accessible to people from all walks of life, among them teachers, psychotherapists, lawyers, businessmen and -women, prisoners, parents, and children. This has helped build a worldwide community of practitioners, both lay and monastic. In India, besides having regular gatherings of practitioners, we hold retreats and 'Days of Mindfulness', especially in the field of education and applied ethics.

Thay's simple yet articulate exposition and explanation of complex concepts makes him an artist with words. His poetry speaks eloquently to our hearts and minds. His deceptively simple teachings help make such simple acts as smiling and conscious breathing into practices of self-calming and of deep seeing.

Shantum Seth
New Delhi
August 2017

INTRODUCTION

Alan Weisman

A few years ago, while researching my book *The World Without Us*, I visited a tribe in Ecuador whose remaining shred of once bountiful Amazon forest was so depleted that they'd resorted to hunting spider monkeys. This was especially grim because they believed themselves to be descended from those very primates. In essence, they'd been reduced to eating their ancestors.

In this new book by Thich Nhat Hanh, *The World We Have*, there is a remarkable corollary, called the Sutra on the Son's Flesh. Its moral is that if we don't consume with mindfulness and compassion, we will in effect be eating our children.

I am neither a Buddhist nor a sage, merely a journalist, so I am humbled to introduce this latest summons to mindful action by Thich Nhat Hanh. I am also gratified that his venerable voice, which during a terrible war once helped our world regain its moral bearings, is raised yet again to guide us in an age of urgent need. In very separate ways, both he and I have concluded that as humans lose the links to the past from which we spring, we threaten to kill our future.

In *The World Without Us,* I imagined how our planet might respond if humans were suddenly extracted. How long would it take the rest of nature to obliterate our deep tracks, undo our damage, replenish our empty niche, subdue our toxins, and soften our scars? As my research revealed, many of our monumental works and seemingly invincible structures would succumb surprisingly quickly. Other matters that we've set in motion, however, such as all the carbon we've exhumed and redeposited in the atmosphere, would take nature much longer to reabsorb.

And yet, nature has all the time in the world. Scientists, materials engineers, and the Buddha concur: nothing we do is permanent.

In fact, our world has been through far greater losses than the one we're currently perpetrating. Periodically, volcanic eruptions that lasted up to a million years and cataclysmic asteroid strikes have so devastated this planet that nearly everything alive was extinguished. Nevertheless, life, so awesomely resilient, is continually reborn in some unexpected and fertile incarnation—filling the Earth in one era with colossal reptiles, in another with magnificent mammals. This mysterious, wondrous life has recycled before, and will again.

Just as no person lives forever, no species escapes eventual extinction, and ours is no exception. Yet to be alive, as Thich Nhat Hanh so eloquently reminds us, is both a blessing and an honour to uphold. To realize that we are part of a grand, changing, living pageant—one that, no matter how deep a wound it sustains, will always be renewed—brings great peace. But this grand perspective doesn't relieve us of the responsibility of living and acting at the highest possible level of awareness while we are here now. On the contrary; in one of those illuminating paradoxes that a Buddhist like Thich Nhat Hanh handles so deftly, the way to achieve enlightened freedom from the confines of the physical realm emerges directly from how consciously we engage with it.

One bright, cold afternoon in November 2003, I stood with five admirably engaged and dedicated fellow humans at the edge of a deep valley. We were north of Gh'orwon in South Korea's Kangwon-do Province, staring at one of the most beautiful and terrifying places on Earth. Below us was the Demilitarized Zone: a buffer four kilometres wide that bisects the entire Korean peninsula. For fifty years it had kept two of the world's largest and most hostile armies from murdering each other.

Even so, each could still clearly see the other's hillside bunkers, bristling with weapons that neither would hesitate to fire if provoked. Compounding this tragedy was the sad irony that these mortal enemies shared the same history, language, and blood.

But they also shared a miracle. After a half-century, the abandoned no-man's-land between them had reverted from rice paddies and villages to wilderness. Inadvertently, it had become one of the most important nature refuges in Asia. Among the imperiled species that depend on it was one revered throughout the Orient: the red-crowned crane. The second-rarest crane on Earth after the whooping crane, it is repeatedly depicted in paintings and silks as a symbol of longevity, and as a manifestation of the noble virtues of Confucian scholars and Buddhist monks. Many, if not most, of these fabulous birds now winter in the DMZ.

My hosts were scientists and staff from the Korean Federation of Environmental Movement. Together, we watched as eleven red-crowned cranes—cherry caps, black extremities, but otherwise as pure and white as innocence itself—silently glided between the seething North and South Korean forces. Placidly, they settled in the bulrushes to feed.

Because only 1,500 of these creatures remain, it was thrilling to see juveniles among them. Privileged as we were to witness this, it was impossible to forget—and even harder to reconcile—that this auspicious setting owed its existence to an unresolved war. If peace were ever restored, developers of suburbs to the south and industrial parks to the north had plans for this place that didn't include wildlife. The reunification of Korea could mean a habitat loss that might shrink the red-crowned cranes' gene pool critically enough to doom the entire species.

Unless, that is, Korean leaders realized that amid the sorrow of this divided land lay a great opportunity. A growing alliance of world scientists, including my hosts, have proposed that the DMZ be declared an international peace park. It would be a gift of life to our Earth, protecting this haven for scores of precious creatures. By preserving the common ground between them, the two Koreas would not only save many irreplaceable species, but also earn immense international good will.

I asked my companions if they thought this would happen.

'We'll never stop trying.'

But three days later I realized the challenge they faced, when one of them took me to a Buddhist temple in the mountains north of Seoul. This was one of the oldest Zen monasteries in Korea, a site that monks and environmentalists alike were fighting to exclude from a plan to ring the swelling capital city with new eight-lane highways—one of which would tunnel directly under this ancient sacred ground.

Outrageous, surely. And yet, I asked the head monk, did their struggle to save this sanctuary conflict with Buddhist principles of non-attachment to material things? For that matter, might the ethos of an environmental activist like my companion, clinging for dear life to the planet he courageously defended, actually be an impediment to his spiritual progress? If Buddhism teaches impermanence, is the impulse to preserve the environment—or anything, for that matter—therefore pointless?

It is true, the monk replied, that our world is impermanent. Yet, he added, just as we need to keep our bodies healthy and pure as we seek enlightenment, while we dwell on this planet we have a duty to cherish and protect it.

I sensed an intricate lesson in this paradox. Before leaving, I had another question for the monk. In a large hall below his quarters where we sat drinking tea, disciples seated on a wooden floor were chanting. I'd glanced in when we arrived; it was adorned with carved dragons and gilded Bodhisattvas. For a while, I'd lingered and listened, not understanding, yet something within me stirred.

'What are they singing?' I asked.

'That is the Diamond Sutra.'

'What does it mean?'

He explained that what appears as form is really emptiness but that emptiness also has form. I didn't quite understand.

'Perhaps you need to listen more.'

In this new book, Thich Nhat Hanh invites us all to listen. He defines the Diamond Sutra as the essence of deep ecology, a description of how nothing exists as an isolated self, because it is dependent upon and connected to everything else. Just as a flower can't exist apart from the sun that energizes it, the soil that nourishes it, the creatures that pollinate it, or from the rain that waters it, we human beings have no existence separate from all else. The Diamond Sutra, Nhat Hanh explains, teaches that to see ourselves only as humans is a sad limitation of our true essence. We descend not just from our human ancestors, but from animal and plant ancestors, and even from the stuff of the Earth itself, its mineral components are our own.

In a passage as unforgettable to me as the temple chanting that still resounds in my memory, Thich Nhat Hanh reminds us that we have been rocks, clouds, and trees. 'We humans are a young species. We have to remember our past existences and be humble.'

The humility he describes is an admonition to respect not just human intelligence, but an orchid's knowledge of how to produce mesmerizing blossoms, or a snail's ability to make a flawless shell. To respect, however, means not merely to bow before the butterfly and the magnolia, or to serenely meditate on an oak's marvels. *The World We Have* is a call to act. Its subtitle—*A Buddhist Approach to Peace and Ecology*—hints that those two are inextricable. Just as two warring Koreas have an opportunity in the flowering ground between them to not only give the world a gift but to draw closer to each other, so, in the epic crisis that threatens to choke our entire planet, do we have a chance to join in a common cause greater than all our imagined differences.

The environment unites every human, of every nation and creed. If we fail to save it, we all perish. If we rise to meet the need, we and all to which ecology binds us—other humans, other species, other everything—survive together. And that will be peace.

PART ONE

A COLLECTIVE AWAKENING

1

THE BELLS OF MINDFULNESS

The bells of mindfulness are calling out to us, trying to wake us up, reminding us to look deeply at our impact on the planet.

~

The bells of mindfulness are sounding. All over the Earth, we are experiencing floods, droughts, and massive wildfires. Sea ice is melting in the Arctic and hurricanes and heat waves are killing thousands. The forests are fast disappearing, the deserts are growing, species are becoming extinct every day, and yet we continue to consume, ignoring the ringing bells.

All of us know that our beautiful green planet is in danger. Our way of walking on the Earth has a great influence on animals and plants. Yet we act as if our daily lives have nothing to do with the condition of the world. We are like sleepwalkers, not knowing what we are doing or where we are heading. Whether we can wake up or not depends on whether we can walk mindfully on our Mother Earth. The future of all life, including our own, depends on our mindful steps. We have to hear the bells of mindfulness that are sounding all across our planet. We have to start learning how to live in a way that a future will be possible for our children and our grandchildren.

I have sat with the Buddha for a long time and consulted him about the issue of global warming, and the teaching of the Buddha is very clear. If we continue to live as we have been living, consuming without a thought of the future, destroying our forests and emitting dangerous amounts of carbon dioxide, then devastating climate change is inevitable. Much of our ecosystem will be destroyed. Sea levels will rise and coastal cities will be inundated, forcing hundreds of millions of refugees from their homes, creating wars and outbreaks of infectious disease.

We need a kind of collective awakening. There are among us men and women who are awakened, but it's not enough; most people are still sleeping. We have constructed a system we can't control. It imposes itself on us, and we become its slaves and victims. For most of us who want to have a house, a car, a refrigerator, a television, and so on, we must sacrifice our time and our lives in exchange. We are constantly under the pressure of time. In former times, we could afford three hours to drink one cup of tea, enjoying the company of our friends in a serene and spiritual atmosphere. We could organize a party to celebrate the blossoming of one orchid in our garden. But today we can no longer afford these things. We say that time is money. We have created a society in which the rich become richer and the poor become poorer, and we are so caught up in our own immediate problems that we cannot afford to be aware of what is going on with the rest of the human family or our planet Earth. In my mind I see a group of chickens in a cage disputing over a few seeds of grain, unaware that in a few hours they will all be killed.

People in China, India, Vietnam, and other developing countries are still dreaming the 'American dream', as if that dream were the ultimate goal of mankind—everyone has to have a car, a bank account, a cell phone, and a television set of their own. In twenty-five years the population of China will be 1.5 billion people, and if each of them wants to drive their own private car, China will need 99 million barrels of oil every day. But world production today is only 84 million barrels per day. So the American dream is not possible for the people of China, India, or Vietnam. The American dream is no longer even possible for the Americans. We can't continue to live like this. It's not a sustainable economy.

We have to have another dream: the dream of brotherhood and sisterhood, of loving kindness and compassion. That dream is possible right here and now. We have the Dharma, we have the means, and we have enough wisdom to be able to live this dream. Mindfulness is at the heart of awakening, of enlightenment. We practise breathing to be able to be here in the present moment so that we can recognize what is happening in us and around us. If what's happening inside us is despair, we have to recognize that and act right away. We may not want to confront that mental formation, but it's a reality, and we have to recognize it in order to transform it.

We don't have to sink into despair about global warming; we can act. If we just sign a petition and forget about it, it won't help much. Urgent action must be taken at the individual and collective levels. We all have a great desire to be able to live in peace and to have environmental sustainability. What most of us don't yet have are concrete ways of making our commitment to sustainable living a reality in our daily lives. We haven't organized ourselves. We can't only blame our governments and corporations for the chemicals that pollute our drinking water, for the violence in our neighborhoods, for the wars that destroy so many lives. It's time for each of us to wake up and take action in our own lives.

We witness violence, corruption, and destruction all around us. We all know that the laws we have in place aren't strong enough to control the superstition, cruelty, and abuses of power that we see daily. Only faith and determination can keep us from falling into deep despair.

Buddhism is the strongest form of humanism we have. It can help us learn to live with responsibility, compassion, and loving kindness. Every Buddhist practitioner should be a protector of the environment. We have the power to decide the destiny of our planet. If we awaken to our true situation, there will be a change in our collective consciousness. We have to help the Buddha to wake up the people who are living in a dream.

2

A GLOBAL ETHIC

The path of brotherhood and sisterhood is more precious than any ideology or religion.

~

Everything, even the Buddha, is always changing and evolving. Thanks to our practice of looking deeply, we can realize that the sufferings of our time are different from those of the time of Siddhartha, and so the methods of practice should also be different. That is why the Buddha inside of us also needs to evolve, so that the Buddha can be relevant to our time.

The Buddha of our time can use a telephone, even a cell phone, but she is free from that cell phone. The Buddha of our time knows how to help prevent ecological damage and global warming; she will not destroy the beauty of the planet or waste all her time competing with other people.

The Buddha of our time wants to offer the world a global ethic so that everyone can agree on a good path to follow. Global harmony isn't possible if we don't have a global ethic. The Buddha of our time wants to restore harmony, cultivate brotherhood and sisterhood, protect all the species of the planet, prevent deforestation, and reduce the emission of toxic gases.

Since you are the continuation of the Buddha, you can help offer the world a path that can prevent the destruction of the ecosystem, one that can reduce the amount of violence and despair. It would be very kind of you to help the Buddha continue to realize what he began 2,600 years ago.

Our planet Earth has a variety of life, and each species depends on all the other species in order to be able to manifest and continue. We're not only outside of each other but we're also inside each other. It is very important to hold the Earth in our arms and in our heart, to preserve the beautiful planet and to protect all species. The Lotus Sutra mentions the name of a special bodhisattva—Dharanimdhara, or Earth Holder as someone who preserves and protects the Earth.

Earth Holder is the energy that is holding us together as an organism. She is a kind of engineer or architect whose task is to create space for us to live in, to build bridges for us to cross from one side to the other, to construct roads so that we can go to the people we love. Her task is to further communication between human beings and the other species and to protect the environment. It is said that when the Buddha tried to visit his mother, Mahamaya, who had passed away, it was Dharanimdhara who built the road on which the Buddha travelled. Although Earth Holder bodhisattva is mentioned in the Lotus Sutra, she doesn't have a chapter of her own. We should recognize this bodhisattva in order to collaborate with her. We should all help to create a new chapter for her, because Earth Holder is so desperately needed in this era of globalization.

When you contemplate an orange, you see that everything in the orange participates in making up the orange. Not only the sections of the orange belong to the orange; the skin and the seeds are also parts of the orange. This is what we call the universal aspect of the orange. Everything in the orange is the orange, but the skin remains the skin, the seed remains the seed, the section of the orange remains the section of the orange. The same is true with our globe. Although we've become a world community, the French continue to be French, the Japanese remain Japanese, the Buddhists remain Buddhists, and the Christians remain Christians. The skin of the orange continues to be the skin, and the sections of the orange continue to be the sections; the sections don't have to be transformed into the skin in order for there to be harmony.

Harmony, however, is impossible if we don't have a global ethic, and the global ethic that the Buddha devised is the Five

Mindfulness Trainings. The Five Mindfulness Trainings are the path we should follow in this era of global crisis because they are the practice of sisterhood and brotherhood, understanding and love, and the practice of protecting ourselves and protecting the planet. The mindfulness trainings are concrete realizations of mindfulness. They are non-sectarian, not bearing the mark of any religion, race, or ideology; their nature is universal. We always say that it's not necessary for people to call themselves Buddhist in order to practise the trainings. You can adopt them as a Christian, a Jew, a Muslim, or as a French, Japanese, Chinese, or American person. Everything that has the capacity of bringing us to awareness, everything that can generate understanding, mutual acceptance, and love, is part of Buddhism, even if Buddhist terms are not there. You may also inspire friends to return to their roots and discover the equivalent of the Five Mindfulness Trainings inherent in their own tradition, whether it is Islam, Judaism, Christianity, or another tradition.

When you practise the Five Mindfulness Trainings, you become a bodhisattva helping to create harmony, protect the environment, safeguard peace, and cultivate brotherhood and sisterhood. Not only do you safeguard the beauties of your own culture, but those of other cultures as well and all the beauties of the Earth. With the Five Mindfulness Trainings in your heart, you are already on the path of transformation and healing.

THE FIVE MINDFULNESS TRAININGS

The First Mindfulness Training

Aware of the suffering caused by the destruction of life, I am committed to cultivating compassion and learning ways to protect the lives of people, animals, plants, and minerals. I am determined not to kill, not to let others kill, and not to support any act of killing in the world, in my thinking, and in my way of life.

The Second Mindfulness Training

Aware of the suffering caused by exploitation, social injustice, stealing, and oppression, I am committed to cultivating loving kindness and learning ways to work for the well-being of people, animals, plants, and minerals. I will practise generosity by sharing my time, energy, and material resources with those who are in real need. I am determined not to steal and not to possess anything that should belong to others. I will respect the property of others, but I will prevent others from profiting from human suffering or the suffering of other species on Earth.

The Third Mindfulness Training

Aware of the suffering caused by sexual misconduct, I am committed to cultivating responsibility and learning ways to protect the safety and integrity of individuals, couples, families, and society. I am determined not to engage in sexual relations without love and a long-term commitment. To preserve the happiness of myself and others, I am determined to respect my commitments and the commitments of others. I will do everything in my power to protect children from sexual abuse and to prevent couples and families from being broken by sexual misconduct.

The Fourth Mindfulness Training

Aware of the suffering caused by unmindful speech and the inability to listen to others, I am committed to cultivating loving speech and deep listening in order to bring joy and happiness to others and relieve others of their suffering. Knowing that words can create happiness or suffering, I am determined to speak truthfully, with words that inspire self-confidence, joy, and hope. I will not spread news that I do not know to be certain and will not criticize or condemn things of which I am not sure. I will refrain from uttering words that can cause division or discord, or that can cause the family or the community to break. I am determined to make all efforts to reconcile and resolve all conflicts, however small.

The Fifth Mindfulness Training

Aware of the suffering caused by unmindful consumption, I am committed to cultivating good health, both physical and mental, for myself, my family, and my society by practising mindful eating, drinking, and consuming. I will ingest only items that preserve peace, well-being, and joy in my body, in my consciousness, and in the collective body and consciousness of my family and society. I am determined not to use alcohol or any other intoxicant or to ingest foods or other items that contain toxins, such as certain TV programmes, magazines, books, films, and conversations. I am aware that to damage my body or my consciousness with these poisons is to betray my ancestors, my parents, my society, and future generations. I will work to transform violence, fear, anger, and confusion in myself and in society by practising a diet for myself and for society. I understand that a proper diet is crucial for self-transformation and for the transformation of society.

In the First Training we vow to cherish all life on Earth and not support any acts of killing. In the Second Training we pledge to practise generosity and not support social injustice and oppression. In the Third Training we make a commitment to behave responsibly in our relationships and not engage in sexual misconduct. The Fourth Training asks us to practise loving speech and deep listening in order to relieve others of their suffering.

The practice of mindful consumption and mindful eating is the object of the Fifth Mindfulness Training. The Fifth Training is the way out of the difficult situation our world is in. When we practice the Fifth Training, we recognize exactly what to consume and what not to consume in order to keep our bodies, our minds, and the Earth healthy and not cause suffering for ourselves and for others. Mindful consumption is the way to heal ourselves and to heal the world. As a spiritual family and as the human family, we can all help avert global warming by following this practice. We should become aware of the presence of the bodhisattva Earth Holder in every one of us. We should become the hands and the arms of Earth Holder in order to be able to act quickly.

You may have heard that God is in us, or that the Buddha is in us. But for most of us this is an abstract notion. We have such a vague idea of what Buddha or God actually is. In the Buddhist tradition, Buddha resides inside us as energy—the energy of mindfulness, the energy of concentration, and the energy of insight—that will bring about understanding, compassion, love, joy, togetherness, and non-discrimination. Some of our friends in the Christian tradition speak of the Holy Ghost or the Holy Spirit as the energy of God. Wherever the Holy Spirit is, there is healing and love. We can speak in the same way of mindfulness, concentration, and insight. The energy of mindfulness, concentration, and insight gives rise to understanding, compassion, forgiveness, joy, transformation, and healing. That is the energy of a Buddha. If you are inhabited by that energy, you are a Buddha, at least for that moment. And that energy can be cultivated and can manifest fully in you.

3

DIET FOR A MINDFUL PLANET

~

The Buddha once told his monks this story:

> *A couple and their young son were crossing a vast desert on their way to seek asylum in another land. But they hadn't planned well and were only halfway across the desert when they ran out of food. Realizing that all three of them would die in the desert, the parents made a horrifying decision: they decided to kill and eat their child. Every morning they ate a morsel of his flesh, just enough for the energy to walk a little further, all the while crying, 'Where is our little boy?' They carried the rest of their son's flesh on their shoulders, so it could continue to dry in the sun. Every night the couple looked at each other and asked, 'Where is our beloved child now?' And they cried and pulled their hair, and beat their chests with grief. Finally, they were able to cross the desert and arrive in the new land.*

When the Buddha was finished with the story, he asked the monks, 'Do you think this couple enjoyed eating their son's flesh?'

'No,' the monks replied. 'These parents suffered terribly when they had to consume their child's body.' And the Buddha said, 'We have to practise eating in such a way that will retain compassion in our heart. We have to eat in mindfulness. Otherwise we will be eating the flesh of our own children.'

In the Sutra on the Son's Flesh, the Buddha teaches us how to practise mindful consumption in order to preserve our future. Our future can always be glimpsed in our present. If the present looks one way, the future will probably look the same, since the future is made of the present. Therefore, in order to safeguard our future, we have to make changes in the present. If we apply the Sutra on the Son's Flesh in our daily lives, we will be able to save ourselves and our planet.

The situation the Earth is in today has been created by unmindful production and unmindful consumption. We are doing violence to our home and we are facing global warming and catastrophic climate changes. We have created an environment that is conducive to violence, hate, discrimination, and despair.

In modern life people think their bodies belong to them, and they can do anything they want to themselves. 'We have the right to live our own lives,' they say. The law supports such a declaration; that is one of the manifestations of individualism. But according to the teaching of the Buddha, your body is not yours. Your body belongs to your ancestors, your parents, and future generations. It also belongs to society and to all the other living beings. All of them have come together—the trees, the clouds, the soil, everything—to bring about the presence of this body. Our bodies are like the Earth. And there is the bodhisattva Earth Holder, holding everything together.

Keeping your body healthy is a way of expressing gratitude and loyalty to the whole cosmos, to all ancestors, and to future generations. If we are healthy, everyone can benefit from it—not only human beings, but animals, plants, and minerals. This is a bodhisattva precept. When we practise the Fifth Mindfulness Training we are already on the path of a bodhisattva.

We are what we consume. If we look deeply into how much and what items we consume every day, we will come to know our own nature very well. We have to eat, drink, and consume, but if we do it unmindfully, we may destroy our body and our consciousness, showing a lack of gratitude toward our ancestors, our parents, and future generations. We all know that sometimes we open the refrigerator and take out an item that is not good for our health. We are intelligent enough to recognize that. But still we go ahead and eat it to try to cover up the uneasiness within ourselves. We consume to forget our worries and our anxieties. The practice recommended by the Buddha is that when a feeling of anxiety or fearfulness comes up, we should not try to suppress it with the method of consumption. Instead, invite the energy of mindfulness to manifest. Practise mindful walking and mindful breathing to generate the energy of mindfulness, and invite that energy up to take care of the energy that's making you suffer. If we don't practice, we don't have enough of the energy of mindfulness to take care of our fear and anger, and that's why we consume to repress those negative energies.

The Buddha recommends that each monk and nun has a bowl with which to go on the almsround. The Buddhist term for the begging bowl is 'the vessel of appropriate measure'. Since the bowl is exactly the right size, we always know just how much to eat. We never overeat, because overeating brings sickness to our bodies. Obesity has become a huge health problem in Western society, while people in poor countries don't get enough to eat every day.* We ignore the rule of moderation. Mindfulness of eating helps us to know what and how much we should eat.

---

*'Industrial agriculture dominated by multinational corporations is largely responsible for creating a skewed global food system in which 1 billion suffer from obesity while 840 million people go hungry.' Eric Holt-Gimenez and Isabella Kenfield, 'When Renewable Isn't Sustainable: Agrofuels and the 2007 Energy Independence and Security Act', *Food First Policy Brief #13*, March 2008.

We should take only what we can eat. I suggest that, for most of us we take less than what we're used to eating every day. We see that people who consume less are healthier and more joyful, and that those who consume a lot may suffer very deeply. If we chew carefully, if we eat only what is healthy, then we will not bring sickness into our body or our mind. We will not eat the flesh of our ancestors, our children, and their children.

When we eat mindfully, we're in close touch with the food. The food we eat comes to us from nature, from living beings, and from the cosmos. To touch it with our mindfulness is to show our gratitude. Eating in mindfulness can be a great joy. We pick up our food with our fork, we look at it for a few moments before putting it into our mouth, and then we chew it carefully and mindfully, at least fifty times. Practising like this, we are in touch with the entire cosmos.

There are types of joy that can be nourishing and healing, bringing us calm, comfort, making us peaceful and fresh, and helping us to remain clear and lucid. That is the kind of joy that we need. There are other kinds of joy that may bring us a lot of suffering later on: the joy of eating unhealthy foods, of drinking alcohol, of eating too many sweets, of bringing toxins into the body. We have to distinguish between the two kinds of joy. One is healing and nourishing and the other is destructive.

The food we eat can reveal the interconnectedness of the universe, the Earth, all living beings, and ourselves. Each bite of vegetable, each drop of soy sauce, each piece of tofu contains the life of the sun and of the Earth. We can see and taste the whole universe in a piece of bread! We can see the meaning and value of life in those precious morsels of food.

Having the opportunity to sit with our family and friends

and enjoy wonderful food is something precious, something not everyone has. Many people in the world are hungry. When I hold a bowl of rice or a piece of bread, I know that I am fortunate, and I feel compassion for all those who have no food to eat and who are without friends or family. This is a very deep practice. We don't need to go to a temple or a church in order to practise this. We can practise it right at our dinner table. With mindful eating we can cultivate the seeds of compassion and understanding that will strengthen our determination to do something to help hungry and lonely people be nourished.

One thing we can do is to consider how much meat we eat. For over 2,000 years, many Buddhists have practised vegetarianism with the purpose of nourishing compassion toward animals. Now we've also discovered that switching to a vegetarian diet may be one of the most effective ways to fight world hunger and global warming. The practice of raising animals for food has created some of the worst environmental damage on the planet and is responsible for one quarter of greenhouse gas emissions.*

Our way of eating and producing food can be very violent to other species, to our own bodies, and to the Earth. Mother Earth suffers deeply because of our way of eating. Animals raised for meat are the world's biggest source of water pollution;

---

*'The livestock sector emerges as one of the top two or three most significant contributors to the most serious environmental problems, at every scale from local to global… Livestock's contribution to environmental problems is on a massive scale, and its potential contribution to their solution is equally large. The impact is so significant that it needs to be addressed with urgency.' United Nations Food and Agriculture Organization (FAO), *Livestock's Long Shadow: Environmental Issues and Options*, 29 November 2006.

waste from factory farms and slaughterhouses flows into our rivers, streams, and drinking water. In the US alone, hundreds of millions of acres of forest have been razed to grow crops to feed livestock. The precious tropical rainforests that keep our planet cool and provide a home for most of the plant and animal species on Earth are being burned and cleared to create grazing land for cattle.

Much of the millions of tons of grain we grow isn't used to feed people but instead to raise cattle for meat and to make alcohol. An Environmental Protection Agency report on US agricultural crop production in the year 2000 states that, according to the National Corn Growers Association, about 80 per cent of all corn grown in the US is consumed by domestic and overseas livestock, poultry, and fish production.* When you hold a piece of meat and look at it deeply, you will see that a huge amount of grain and water has been used to make that one piece of meat. A tremendous amount of grain and water is also used to make alcohol. Tens of thousands of children die of starvation and malnutrition every day; that grain could feed them. When we drink alcohol with mindfulness, we see that we are drinking the blood of our children. We're eating our children, our mother, and our father. We are eating up the Earth.

We have to put pressure on the livestock industry to change. If we stop consuming, they will stop producing. By eating meat we share responsibility for causing climate change, the destruction of our forests, and the poisoning of our air and water. The simple act of becoming a vegetarian can make a difference in the health of our planet. If you're not able to entirely stop

---

*www.epa.gov/oecaagct/agloi/cropmajor.html.

eating meat, you can still decide to make an effort to cut back. By cutting meat out of your diet ten or even five days a month, you will already be performing a miracle—a miracle that will help solve the problem of hunger in the developing world and dramatically reduce greenhouse gases.

With each meal, we make choices that help or harm Mother Earth. 'What shall I eat today?' is a very deep question. You might want to ask yourself that question every morning. You may find that as you practise mindful consumption and begin to look deeply at what you eat and drink, your desire for meat and for alcohol will diminish.

In many Buddhist traditions, monks and nuns are vegetarian. Many lay Buddhist practitioners in China and Vietnam are also vegetarian, and there are others who refrain from eating meat ten days a month. I urge everyone to at least to reduce their meat eating by half. During my most recent visits to the United States, many American Buddhist practitioners told me they had made the commitment to stop eating meat or to eat fifty per cent less meat. This is a collective awakening that's already taking place. If we can make the commitment to become vegetarian, or partially vegetarian, we'll feel a sense of well-being—we'll have peace, joy, and happiness right from the moment we make this vow. Our collective awakening can create worldwide change.

We have to practise mindful consumption to protect ourselves, our families, our society, and the planet. Children, teachers, and parents can all practise mindful consumption. Leaders of organizations and communities can practise mindful consumption and encourage others to follow their example. If you were the mayor of a city, you'd want to protect the people in your city from the unmindful consumption that will bring more violence and suffering to your town. Even the president of the most powerful nation in the world can be encouraged to consume more mindfully. Even the president has Buddha nature—the seed of understanding and compassion—somewhere in him.

When we're able to get out of the shell of our small self and see that we are interrelated with everyone and everything, we see that each of our acts affects the whole of humankind, the whole cosmos. Keeping your body healthy is an act of kindness toward your ancestors, your parents, future generations, and society. Health is not only bodily health, but also mental health. Mindful consumption brings about health and healing, for ourselves and for our planet.

There are other kinds of things we consume besides food, and mindful consumption encompasses these things as well. In the Discourse on the Four Kinds of Nutriments, the Buddha speaks of food as only one of four sources of our consumption. The second source is called sensory impressions. We consume through our eyes, ears, nose, body, and consciousness. When we look at a film, when we read a magazine article, when we see an advertisement, when we listen to a conversation, we consume.

Sometimes what we consume is relaxing music, fresh garden smells, or the beauty of the world around us. But often what we consume contains a lot of toxins. When you drive through the city, you consume—the advertisements you see penetrate you. When you have a conversation with someone whose words are full of hate and violence, these words stay with you. By the time the average child in the US has finished elementary school, she has watched over 8,000 murders and over 100,000 violent acts on television.* That's a lot of toxic consumption already in a small child's body. All the poisons we ingest into our body and our consciousness destroy the body and consciousness transmitted to us by our parents and our ancestors.

To illustrate our sensory consumption, the Buddha told the story of a cow with skin disease. The skin disease was so severe the cow had lost some of her skin, leaving her vulnerable to all the insects that came to suck her blood or eat her flesh. The cow had no means of protecting herself. When she was brought near an ancient tree, all the tiny creatures living in the bark of the tree would crawl or fly out to land on the cow. When the cow lay down, the tiny beings living in the soil would come up and fix themselves on the cow. And when the cow was brought to the water, the small creatures in the water would come out to eat and suck the blood of the cow. Without mindfulness, we're like a cow without skin, and we allow many toxins to penetrate us and destroy us.

The third nutriment we consume is the food of our intentions or volition. This is our deepest intention, what we want to do with our life. Our desire to do something can give us a great deal of energy. The Buddha gives a very clear example:

> *There's a young man in good health who lives in a town. Outside the town there's a big pit full of very hot coals. If anyone were to fall into that pit, they'd be very badly burned. They'd suffer a lot and could die. One day two very strong men try to pull this young man towards the pit. He doesn't want to go there. He knows that if he goes into that pit he*

---

*Dr Norman Herr, *The Sourcebook for Teaching Science*, San Francisco: Jossey-Bass, 2008.

will suffer incredibly and could even die. But the strongmen are pulling him in that direction.

Those two strongmen are pulling at us; they represent our craving. If we want to be famous, that intention can be very strong and can pull us toward a pit that's full of suffering. It's the same if we want to have honour or praise. A craving for sex can also pull us toward that pit, and can create a lot of suffering. If we have a craving for making money, that craving can pull us along. Our craving consumes us, leaving no room for awareness or mindfulness.

The fourth kind of nutriment we consume is the food of consciousness. This refers to the whole of our consciousness—not just our conscious mind, but our unconscious mind as well. This is the Buddha's story about the food of consciousness:

A criminal had been sentenced to death. The king ordered his soldiers to catch and arrest him and bring him back to the town. When this had been done, the soldiers asked the king what they should do with the criminal. The king said, 'In the morning, take him outside and stab him 100 times.' So that's what they did. Later the king asked them, 'What about the criminal? Did you stab him 100 times?' They answered, 'Yes, your majesty, but he didn't die.' So the king said, 'Take him out again at midday and stab him 100 times.' When they'd done this, the king asked, 'What happened?' The soldiers answered, 'He didn't die.' So the king said, 'Take him out in the evening and stab him 100 times.'

Maybe at that point, he died. The sutra doesn't say. The Buddha asked, 'What do you think, monks? Did that man suffer?' And the monks said, 'Lord Buddha, to be stabbed 100 times is unbearable suffering. But 300 times—we can't imagine.'

We've been stabbed many times in the deep levels of our consciousness. Even before the human species was around there had already been a lot of suffering on Earth. This is what Buddhism calls the First Noble Truth, that life involves suffering, *dukkha*. Whether it is sickness, anger, despair, or depression, we can call it by this name. All the suffering that our ancestors experienced is within us. That kind of suffering is what the Buddha is talking about when the criminal is stabbed so many times. It continues in our daily life. We are hurt by what someone has said and feel they have stabbed us. And our own thoughts may stab us hundreds of times each day.

Yet our suffering is not just our suffering. This is part of Buddhism's Second Noble Truth. It's the suffering of all previous generations, human and non-human. It's also the suffering of the collective consciousness of our own time. We have our genetic heritage, but we also inter-are with all the species alive with us now on this planet. We may not live in a war zone, but in the deepest levels of our consciousness we receive the effects of the suffering of the people who live where there is war. In our conscious mind we may never be aware of it, but our unconscious mind is aware of the suffering that's happening everywhere.

When you suffer it's useful to recognize where your suffering comes from—whether it's from the collective consciousness, your genetic heritage, or from something someone said to you just a moment before. So long as we think 'that person is to blame for my suffering', then it's very difficult for us to transform. If we think that global warming is to blame for our suffering, and we don't see our genetic heritage and all the other factors, then it's difficult to transform that suffering. But if we see our suffering as part of a greater consciousness, then it eases our own individual pain, and our suffering can cease. This is the Third Noble Truth, well-being.

The Fourth Noble Truth of Buddhism is that our suffering can end through our following a mindful path. If we as the human race don't practise mindful consumption of the four kinds of nutriments, we can't save our planet. We need the enlightenment, not just of one person, but the collective enlightenment of the entire human race. Our practice should produce that collective awakening. Each of us has to touch the Buddha inside us every day, so that awakening can manifest in us and in the people around us. Only awakening can save our planet.

4

NATURE AND NON-VIOLENCE

~

Suppose we take a seed of corn and plant it in the damp soil. A week or so later the seed will sprout. About three days later, we may come and ask the corn seedling, 'Dear plant, do you remember the time you were still a seed?' The plant may have forgotten, but because we've been observing, we know that the young cornstalk has truly come from the seed.

When we look at the plant, we no longer see the seed, so we may think the seed has died. But the seed has not died; it has become the plant. If you're capable of seeing the corn seed in the corn plant, you have the kind of wisdom the Buddha called the wisdom of non-discrimination. You don't discriminate between the seed and the plant. You see that they inter-are with each other, that they are the same thing. You can't take the seed out of the plant, and you can't take the plant out of the seed. Looking deeply at the young cornstalk, you can see the seed of corn, still alive, but with a new appearance. The plant is the continuation of the seed.

The practice of meditation helps us to see things other people can't see. We look deeply and we see that father and son, father and daughter, mother and son, mother and daughter, corn seed and cornstalk, have a very close relationship. That is why we should practise to awaken to the fact, to the truth, that we inter-are. The suffering of one is the suffering of the other. If Muslim and Christian, Hindu and Muslim, Israeli and Palestinian, realize they are brother and sister to one other, that the suffering of one side is also the suffering of the other side, then their wars will stop. When we see that we and all living beings are made of the same nature, how can there be division between us? How can there be lack of harmony? When we realize our interbeing nature, we'll stop blaming and exploiting and killing, because we'll know that we inter-are. That is the great awakening we must have in order for the Earth to be saved.

We human beings have always singled ourselves out from the rest of the natural world. We classify other animals and living beings as 'nature', a thing apart from us, and we act as if we're somehow separate from it. Then we ask, 'How should we deal with nature?' We should deal with nature the same way we should deal with ourselves: non-violently. Human beings and nature are inseparable. Just as we should not harm ourselves, we should not harm nature. To harm nature is to harm ourselves, and vice versa.

Causing harm to other human beings causes harm to ourselves. Accumulating wealth and owning excessive portions of the world's natural resources deprives fellow humans of the chance to live. Participating in oppressive and unjust social systems creates and deepens the gap between rich and poor, and aggravates the situation of social injustice. We tolerate excess, injustice, and war, unaware that the human race suffers as a family. While the rest of the human family suffers and starves, the enjoyment of false security and wealth is a delusion.

It's clear that the fate of each individual is inextricably linked to the fate of the whole human race. We must let others live if we ourselves want to live. The only alternative to coexistence is co-non-existence. A civilization in which we must kill and exploit others in order to live is not a healthy civilization. To create a healthy civilization, all must have equal access to education, work, food, shelter, world citizenship, clean air and water, and the ability to circulate freely and settle on any part of the earth. Political and economic systems that deny someone these rights harm the whole human family. Awareness of what is happening to the human family is necessary to repair the damage done already.

To bring about peace within the human family, we must work for harmonious coexistence. If we continue to shut ourselves off from the rest of the world, imprisoning ourselves in narrow concerns and immediate problems, we're not likely to make peace or to survive. The human race is part of nature. We need to have this insight before we can have harmony between people. Cruelty and disruption destroy the harmony of the human family and destroy nature. Among the healing measures needed is legislation that is nonviolent to ourselves and to nature, and that helps prevent us from being disruptive and cruel.

Each individual and all of humanity are part of nature and should be able to live in harmony with nature. Nature can be cruel and disruptive. But we need to treat nature the same way we treat ourselves as individuals and as a human family. If we try to dominate or oppress nature, it rebels. We must be deep friends with nature in order to manage certain aspects of it and create harmony with our environment. This requires a full understanding of nature. Typhoons, tornadoes, droughts, floods, volcanic eruptions, proliferations of harmful insects all constitute a danger to life. We can largely prevent the destruction that natural disasters cause by working with the land from the beginning, and making plans and building decisions that take into account the nature of the land, instead of trying to impose complete control over it with dams, deforestation, and other devices and policies that in the end cause more damage.

One example of what happens when we try to overly control nature is our excessive use of pesticides, which indiscriminately kills many insects and birds and upsets the ecological balance. Economic growth that devastates nature by polluting and exhausting non-renewable resources renders the Earth impossible for beings to live on. Such economic growth may appear to temporarily benefit some humans, but in reality it disrupts and destroys nature as a whole.

The harmony and equilibrium within the individual, society, and nature are being destroyed. Individuals are sick, society is sick, and nature is sick. We must re-establish harmony and equilibrium, but how? Where can we begin the work of healing—in the individual, society, or the environment? We must work in all three domains. People of different disciplines tend to stress their particular area. For example, politicians consider an effective rearrangement of society to be necessary for the salvation of humans and nature and therefore urge that everyone engage in the struggle to make changes in the political system.

Buddhist monks are like psychotherapists in that we tend to look at the problem from the viewpoint of mental health. Meditation aims at creating harmony and equilibrium in the life of the individual. Buddhist meditation deals with both the body and the mind, using breathing as a tool to calm and harmonize the whole human being. As in any therapeutic practice, the patient is placed in an environment that favours the restoration of harmony. Usually psychotherapists spend their time observing and then advising their patient. However, I know of some, who, like monks, observe themselves first, recognizing the need to first free themselves from the fears, anxieties, and despair that exist in each of us. Many therapists seem to think they themselves have no mental problems, but the monk recognizes in himself his susceptibility to fears and anxieties, and to the mental illness caused by the inhumanity of our existing social and economic systems.

Buddhist practitioners believe that the interconnected nature of the individual, society, and the physical environment will reveal itself to us as we recover and we will gradually cease to be possessed by anxiety, fear, and the dispersion of our mind. Among the three domains—individual, society, nature—it is the individual who begins to effect change. But in order to effect change, the individual must be whole. Since this requires an environment favourable to healing, the individual must seek a lifestyle that is free from destructiveness. Our efforts to change ourselves and to change the environment are both necessary, but one can't happen without the other. We know how difficult it is to change the environment if individuals aren't in a state of equilibrium. Our mental health requires that the effort for us to recover our humanness should be given priority.

Restoring mental health does not mean simply adjusting oneself to the modern world of rapid economic growth. The world is sick, and adapting to an unwell environment cannot bring real health. Many people who need psychotherapy are really victims of modern life which separates us from each other and from the rest of the human family. One way to help is to move to a rural area where we have the chance to cultivate the land, grow our own food, wash our clothes in a clear river, and live simply, sharing the same life as that of millions of peasants around the world.

For therapy to be effective, we need environmental change. Political activities are one recourse, but they are not the only one. Tranquilizing ourselves with over consumption is not the way. The poisoning of our ecosystem, the exploding of bombs, the violence in our neighbourhoods and in society, the pressures of time, noise, and pollution, the lonely crowds—all of these have been created by the course of our economic growth and they are all sources of mental illness. Whatever we can do to bring these causes to an end is preventive medicine.

Keeping our mental health as a number one priority means we must also recognize our responsibility to the entire human family. We must work to prevent others from becoming ill at the same time that we safeguard our own humanness. Whether we are monks, nuns, teachers, therapists, artists, carpenters, or politicians, we are human beings too. If we don't apply to ourselves what we try to teach to others, we will become mentally ill. If we just continue on with our lives, going along with the status quo, we gradually become victims of fear, anxiety, and egotism.

A tree reveals itself to an artist when the artist can establish a certain relationship with it. Someone who is not human enough may look at his fellow humans and not see them, may look at a tree and not see it. Many of us can't see things because we're not wholly ourselves. When we're wholly ourselves, we can see how one person, by living fully, can demonstrate to all of us that life is possible, that a future is possible. But the question, 'Is a future possible?' is meaningless if we're not able to see the millions of our fellow humans who suffer, live, and die around us. Only after we've really seen them are we able to see ourselves and see nature.

Recall the Indian Ocean tsunami of 2004, which killed hundreds of thousands of people in Indonesia, Sri Lanka, Thailand, India, and Africa. People who had come from Europe,

Australia, and the United States on vacation also died in the tsunami. All of us suffered all over the world, and we asked the question, why? Why did God allow such a thing to happen? Why did these people have to die? I also suffered. But I practised. I sat down and I practised looking deeply. And what I saw is that when these people died, we also died with them, because we inter-are with them.

You know that when your beloved dies, a part of you also dies; somehow you die with your beloved. That's easy to understand. So if we have understanding and compassion, then when we see other people dying, even strangers on the other side of the world, we suffer and die with them. What we find out is that they die for us. So we have to live for them. We have to live in such a way that the future will be possible for our children and their children. Whether or not their deaths will have meaning depends on our way of living. That is the insight of interbeing. They are us and we are them. When they die, we also die. When we continue to live, they continue to live with us. With that insight, you suffer less and you know how to continue. You carry all of them inside of you and, knowing this, you have peace.

To practise mindfulness and look deeply into the nature of things is to discover their true nature, the nature of interbeing. We find peace and can generate the strength we need in order to be in touch with everything. With this understanding, we can easily sustain the work of loving and caring for the Earth and for each other for a long time.

5

OVERCOMING FEAR

New cells are born every day and old cells die, but they have neither funerals nor birthdays.

~

The Buddha taught that everything is impermanent; that nothing is an absolute entity that remains the same. When we keep that insight in mind, we can see more deeply into the nature of reality, and we won't be trapped in the notion that we're only this body or this life span.

The life of a civilization is like the life of a human being. There is birth and there is death. And this civilization of ours will have to end one day. But we have a huge role to play in determining when it ends and how quickly. If the human race continues on its present course, the end of our civilization is coming sooner than we think. The way we drive our cars, the way we consume, and the way we exploit and destroy the planet's natural resources are speeding up the end of our civilization. Global warming may be an early symptom of that death. If we continue consuming in the way we have, the majority of the planet's human beings may die and our ecosystem will be damaged to such an extent that it will be difficult to support human life as we know it. The world has known many other civilizations before ours, and many civilizations have already perished. Everything is impermanent.

All things are in endless transformation and without an independent self. Intellectually, we may know this, but in reality impermanence is still hard for us to accept. We want the things and the people we love to stay the same.

Understanding impermanence isn't a matter of words or concepts. It's a matter of practise. Only through a daily practise of stopping and looking deeply can we experience and accept the truth of impermanence. We may need to say to ourselves, 'Breathing in, I am looking deeply at some object. Breathing out, I observe the impermanent nature of that object.' The object we're observing might be a flower, a leaf, or a living being. Looking at this object deeply, we can see the change taking place in every instant.

There are two kinds of impermanence. The first is called 'impermanence in every instant'. The second kind of impermanence is when something reaches the end of a cycle of arising, duration, and cessation, and there's a marked change. This is called 'cyclic impermanence'. When we put water on to boil, the water keeps getting hotter and hotter, but there's little discernable change until it actually starts to boil and produce steam. This is the first kind of impermanence, 'impermanence in every instant'. Then, suddenly, we see steam. That's an example of cyclic impermanence. Another example is when a child experiences a growth spurt. Many small changes have been taking place, but we tend not to notice until there's a cyclic change.

We have to look deeply at cyclic change to be able to accept it as a necessary part of life and not be surprised or suffer so greatly when it occurs. We look deeply at the impermanence of our own body, the impermanence of the things around us, the impermanent nature of the people we love, and the impermanent nature of those who cause us to suffer. If we don't look deeply at impermanence, we may think of it as a negative aspect of life because it takes away from us the things we love. But looking deeply, we see that impermanence is neither negative nor positive. It is just impermanence. Without impermanence, life wouldn't be possible. Without impermanence, how could we hope to transform our suffering and the suffering of our loved ones into happiness? Without impermanence, how can we hope to change the destructive path we've set for the Earth?

Impermanence also means interdependence. There's no independent individual phenomenon because everything is changing all the time. A flower is always receiving non-flower elements such as water, air, and sunshine, and it's always giving something back to the environment. A flower is a stream of change, and a person is also a stream of change. At every instant, there's input and output. A flower is always being born and always dying, always connected to the environment around it. The components of the universe depend on one another for their existence.

The example of a wave and water is often given to help us understand the non-self nature of all that exists. A wave can be high or low, can arise or disappear, but the essence of the wave—water—is neither high nor low, neither arising nor disappearing. All signs—high, low, arising, disappearing—cannot touch the essence of water. We cry and laugh according to the sign because we haven't yet seen the essence—that is, the very nature of everything that is. And this is the reality of ourselves. If we only see the wave with its manifestations of being born and dying, we will suffer. But if we see the water, which is the basis of the wave, and we see that all the waves are returning to water, we have nothing to fear.

'Breathing in, I see the nature of impermanence. Breathing out, I see the nature of impermanence.' We have to practise this many times. Because life and reality are impermanent, we feel insecure. The teaching on living deeply in the present moment is what we have to learn and practice to face this feeling of insecurity.

When we begin this practice, we want things to be permanent and we think things have a separate self. Whenever things change, we suffer. To help us not suffer, the Buddha gave us the truths of impermanence and non-self as keys. When we look deeply at the impermanent and non-self nature of all things, we're using those keys to open the door to reality, or *nirvana*. Then our fear and our suffering disappear, and we do not mind whether we are young or old, or even alive or dead. We realize that we do not die in the usual sense of having existed and then ceasing to exist. We see that all life is an ongoing transformation. Impermanence, non-self, and nirvana are the Three Dharma Seals, the mark of any true Buddhist teaching.

When we fight against the nature of impermanence, we suffer. We can allow our fear, anger, and despair to overwhelm us. That's why it is very important to deal with our fear and despair before we can deal with the issue of global warming and other environmental concerns. The Buddha is very clear about this: we have to heal ourselves first before we can heal the planet.

If we don't recognize the fear inside us, it will continue to shape our behavior. The practice offered by the Buddha is not to try to run away from fear. Instead we can invite the fear up into our consciousness, embrace it with our mindfulness, and look deeply into it. Practising like this brings acceptance and understanding. We're no longer pulled along blindly by our fear.

The fear of dying is always there deep down in our consciousness. When someone realizes that they have to die, they may initially revolt against the truth. I have seen this in close friends who have been diagnosed with AIDS or cancer. They refuse to believe it, they struggle with themselves for a long time. When they finally do find acceptance, in that moment they find peace. When we find peace, we relax, and sometimes we even have a chance to overcome our sickness. I have known people with cancer who have been able to survive ten, twenty, even thirty years after their diagnosis, because of their capacity to accept and to live peacefully.

There is a nun who lives in Hanoi, the capital of Vietnam, who was diagnosed with cancer. Her doctor told her she had only a few more months left to live. So she decided to come to Plum Village and live with us before returning home to die. She had totally accepted that the end of her life was near. When she arrived in Plum Village, one of the sisters proposed that she visit a doctor to get another opinion about her cancer. She said, 'No, I didn't come to see a doctor. I've come to spend a few months with you all.'

She lived wholeheartedly every moment of the three months she had with us. She enjoyed walking meditation, sitting meditation, Dharma talks, and Dharma discussion. Three months passed and her visa was about to expire and she had to return to Vietnam. One of the sisters again suggested she go to a doctor 'just to see' what had happened to her cancer. This time she agreed. The doctor told her the metastis had stopped and the cancer had almost disappeared. It's been more than fourteen years since she left Plum Village and she is healthier than ever. So the fact that you accept is very important. Acceptance of death will bring you peace, and with that peace you can sometimes continue to live.

A rising wave has a lot of joy. When the wave is falling, there may be some anxiety about the ending of the wave. Rising always brings about falling. Birth gives rise to death. But if the wave practises meditation and realizes she is water, she can collapse and tumble with joy. She may die as a wave, but she will always be alive as water. The teaching of the Buddha helps us to touch our true nature and receive the insight that will dissipate all kinds of fear. It is possible to die smiling, without fear, without anger.

A drop of rain falling on the ground disappears in no time at all. But it is still there somehow; even if it is absorbed into the soil, it's still there in another form. If it evaporates, it's still there in the air. It's become vapour; you don't see the drop of rain, but that doesn't mean it's no longer there. A cloud can never die. A cloud can become rain or snow or ice, but a cloud cannot become nothing. To die means from something we become nothing, from being we pass into non-being. That is our idea of death. But meditation helps us to touch our true nature of no-birth and no-death. Before the cloud manifests as a cloud, the cloud has been water vapour, has been the ocean. So it has not come from non-being into being. Our notion of birth is just a notion. Our notion of death is just a notion.

That insight is very important; it removes fear. When we understand that we cannot be annihilated, we are liberated from fear. It is an immense relief. With non-fear, true happiness is possible and so is peace. And if you are at peace, our civilization may also find peace. If all of us panic, then we accelerate the death of our civilization. When we have peace, it's much easier for us to handle difficult situations.

The Buddha has taught us to practise looking directly into our seeds of fear, instead of trying to cover them up or run away from them. We have the seed of fear. We are afraid of dying, of being abandoned, of getting sick. We try to forget. We stay busy so we can forget. But the fact is that one day we have to die, we have to be sick, we have to let go of everything. So the Buddha urged the monks and nuns to practise recognizing the seed of fear every day.

This is the practice of the Five Remembrances, designed to help us recognize fear and practise sitting with it. One of the remembrances is, 'I am of the nature to die. I cannot escape death.' You face the truth. You bring the seed of fear up and you face it and embrace it with your mindfulness. This needs courage. By doing this you reduce the strength of the fear and the seed of fear becomes weaker. The practice helps us to accept old age, sickness, and death as realities, facts that we cannot escape. After we have accepted this, we feel much better. When we're struck by a disease like cancer or AIDS we revolt, we say, 'Why me?' Denial is the first reaction. We don't believe it to be the truth. We deny the truth. Then we go through despair and revolt; we struggle with ourselves for a long time. And finally we accept it. In that moment we find peace. And when we find peace, we are more relaxed and we have a chance to overcome the sickness. We have to learn to accept the end of this civilization of ours. If we can accept it, we will be more peaceful. We accept our own death, we accept the death of our civilization. We touch the truth of impermanence and then we have peace. When we have peace, there will be hope again. With this kind of peace we can make use of the technology that is available to us to save this planet of ours. With fear and despair we're not going to be able to save our planet, even if we have the technology to do it. It's possible to die peacefully, with love, if we have the insight of interbeing in us and we know how to touch our true nature of no-birth and no-death.

THE FIVE REMEMBRANCES

I am of the nature to grow old.
There is no way to escape growing old.

I am of the nature to have ill health.
There is no way to escape having ill health.

I am of the nature to die.
There is no way to escape death.

All that is dear to me and everyone
I love are of the nature to change.
There is no way to escape being
separated from them.

I inherit the results of my actions of body, speech, and mind.
My actions are my continuation.

The practice of mindful breathing can help you to look deeply into the nature and roots of your fear. Because of this, I recommend practising the Five Remembrances as a breathing exercise:

Breathing in, I know I am of the nature to grow old.
Breathing out, I know I cannot escape old age.

Breathing in, I know that I am of the nature to get sick.
Breathing out, I know that I cannot escape sickness.

Breathing in, I know that I am of the nature to die.
Breathing out, I know that I cannot escape dying.

Breathing in, I know that one day I will have to let go of
everything and everyone I cherish.

Breathing out, there is no way to bring them along.

Breathing in, I know that I take nothing with me except my actions, thoughts, and deeds.
Breathing out, only my actions come with me.

This practice helps us to accept old age, sickness, and death as realities—facts that we cannot escape. When we can practise accepting these essential truths in this way, we'll have peace and the capacity to live healthy and compassionate lives, no longer causing suffering to ourselves and to others.

If we accept the death of our own human bodily form, we can perhaps begin to accept the eventual death of our own civilization. This civilization of ours is just one civilization, and one day it will have to die in order to make room for another civilization to arise. Many civilizations have already come and gone. Global warming may be an early symptom of the death of our current civilization. If we don't know how to stop our over-consumption, then the death of our civilization will surely come more quickly. We can slow this process by stopping and being mindful, but the only way to do this is to accept the eventual death of this civilization, just as we accept the death of our own physical form. Acceptance is made possible when we know that deep down our true nature is the nature of no-birth and no-death.

Breathing in, I know that this civilization is going to die.
Breathing out, this civilization cannot escape dying.

Once we can accept it, we will not react with anger, denial, and despair any more. Acceptance will bring peace, and if you have peace in you, civilization might have a chance. In your sitting, in your walking, and in your reflection, stop and look deeply in order to have this insight—not as a verbal expression, but as a real insight. This insight will generate mindfulness and peace, acceptance and non-fear, and with that you can make a real contribution.

Scientists tell us that we have enough technology to save our planet. We have renewable energy sources like wind, solar, wave, and geothermal power, and we have access to hybrid, electric, and vegetable oil-powered vehicles. Yet we don't take advantage of this new technology. We're in a state of despair, anger, division, and discrimination. We are not peaceful or awake enough. We don't have enough time; we're too busy. We are unable to collaborate. Technology has to be supported by brotherhood, sisterhood, understanding, and compassion. The technological has to work hand-in-hand with the spiritual. Our spiritual life is the element that can bring about the energies of peace, calm, brotherhood, understanding, and compassion. Without that, our planet doesn't stand a chance.

So the wisdom offered by the Buddha is that we accept impermanence—our own death and the inevitable death of our civilization. And after having accepted that, we will have peace and strength and an awakening that will bring us together. No more hate, no more discrimination. Then we'll have the opportunity to make use of the technology that is available to us in order to save our beloved planet.

If we as members of the human race practise meditation, we can transcend our fear, despair, and forgetfulness. Meditation is not an escape. It is the courage to look at reality with mindfulness and concentration. Meditation is essential for our survival, our peace, our protection. In fact, it is our misperceptions and wrong views that are at the base of our suffering. Throwing away wrong views is the most important, most urgent thing for us to do. Our world needs wisdom and insight. As a teacher, a parent, a journalist, a filmmaker, you are capable of sharing your insights so that you can wake up your country and your people. If your people are awake, then your government will have to act according to the insight of the people. If we practise, we can nurture the dimension of non-fear, of brotherhood and sisterhood.

We don't need to go out and find something to meditate about. The object of our meditation is not something outside of our daily life. The way proposed by the Buddha is to help yourself and to help the people around you; it is to practise looking more deeply in order to be liberated from the notions that are at the foundation of hate, fear, and violence. That is how a collective change of consciousness will come about.

PART TWO

OUR MESSAGE IS OUR ACTION

6

A BEAUTIFUL CONTINUATION

~

When we look at an orange tree we see that season after season it spends its life producing beautiful green leaves, fragrant blossoms, and sweet oranges. These are the best things an orange tree can create and offer to the world. Human beings also make offerings to the world every moment of our daily lives, in the form of our thoughts, our speech, and our actions. We may want to offer the world the best kinds of thought, speech, and action that we can—because they are our continuation, whether we want it to be so or not. We can use our time wisely, generate the energies of love, compassion, and understanding, say beautiful things, inspire, forgive, and act to protect and help the Earth and each other. In this way, we can ensure a beautiful continuation.

The French philosopher Jean-Paul Sartre said that man is the sum of his actions. This is very similar to our Fourth Remembrance: we have to give up everything and everyone we love. All we take with us and all we leave behind are the fruits of our thought, speech, and action during our lifetime. That is our karma, our continuation. When a cloud is polluted, the rain is polluted. Purifying thoughts, words, and actions create a beautiful continuation.

Buddhism uses the word 'karma.' Karma is action—action as cause and action as effect. When action is a cause, we call it *karmahetu*. That thought, speech, or act will have an effect on our mental and physical health and on the health of the world. And that effect, bitter or sweet, wholesome or unwholesome, is the fruit of the karma, the fruit of the thought—*karmaphala*. We are continued into the future through the effects of our thoughts, speech, and actions.

Thought and speech are forms of action. When we produce

a thought that is full of anger, fear, or despair, it has an immediate effect on our health and on the health of the world. Painful thoughts can be very powerful, affecting our bodies, our minds, and the world. We should make an effort not to produce these kinds of thoughts too often. If you've said something that's not worthy of you, say something else today, and that will transform everything. A positive thought will bring us physical and mental health, and it will help the world to heal itself.

Right speech, as recommended by the Buddha, inspires understanding, joy, hope, brotherhood, and sisterhood. We may say something that expresses our loving kindness, our non-discrimination, and our willingness to bring relief. Uttering such words makes us feel better in body and mind. Speaking such words several times a day will bring healing and transformation to ourselves, to others, and to the world. Everyone benefits.

The Buddha advises right action because that action will have an effect on our physical and mental health as well as that of the world. We can kill a person, an animal, a tree. Or we can protect a person, an animal, a tree. We have to ensure that our actions are in the direction of Right Action. When we perform a physical act that has the power to protect, save, support, or bring relief, that act brings an element of healing to us and to the world. When you are full of compassion, even if you don't take action your compassion will generate change. Compassion, by its nature, generates compassionate action.

Thoughts, speech, and actions create karma, and we produce this energy of karma every moment of our daily life. Every thought, word, and act carries our signature. That is your continuation, and it is never lost. It is naive to think that after the disintegration of this body there will be nothing left. When we observe deeply, we see that nothing is really born and nothing can really die. Our true nature is the nature of no-birth and no-death. When we practise meditation, we can see this.

The Buddha spoke of the impermanence of things, and many other thinkers have also spoken of impermanence. The sixth-century Greek philosopher Heraclitus said we can never step into the same river twice, because the river is constantly changing. Nothing stays the same for two consecutive moments. A view that is not based on impermanence is a wrong view. When we have the insight of impermanence, we suffer less and we create more happiness.

This is not just philosophy; it is the way things are. When you are angry with your friend, and you are about to have an argument, the Buddha would say to you, 'Close your eyes. Imagine yourself and your friend in three centuries. Where will the two of you be?' When you can see where you'll be three hundred years from now, you see that it's not wise to argue, because life is impermanent. If you can touch impermanence, then when you open your eyes you will no longer be angry and the only thing that makes sense at that moment is to open your arms and hug that person.

Perhaps you agree intellectually that things are impermanent, but in your day-to-day life, you act as if things are permanent. Impermanence is not a theory or philosophy; it's a practice. We should practise the concentration on impermanence. Looking at a flower, you see that it is impermanent. Looking at a person, you see that he or she is impermanent. All day long, wherever you look, whatever you hear and see, concentrate on it with the insight on impermanence. It is the concentration on impermanence that will save you, and not the idea of impermanence. With mindfulness we can keep the insight of impermanence alive and that will protect us from producing wrong thinking or wrong speech.

Our karma, our actions, continues us. Its manifestation has already started. Our life is a manifestation of our karma, and we can make that manifestation beautiful and meaningful and it will have a good influence on other manifestations now and in the future. If we know how to create the energy of love, understanding, compassion, and beauty, then we can contribute a lot to the world, positively influencing other manifestations. We don't have to wait until our bodies decompose for our continuation to begin. If the manifestations occurring in the present moment are beautiful and good, their continuation will be also beautiful and good.

When we look into our bodies and our consciousness we see that we are a complex organism. There are so many species, so many elements that can be found in our body and in our consciousness. In every cell we can see the whole history of humanity of the Earth, and the cosmos. Each cell in our body is capable of giving us all kinds of data and information concerning the cosmos. A single cell can tell us a lot about our ancestors; not only human but also our animal, plant, and mineral ancestors. Every time we make a step during walking meditation, we are moving like an organism, we are moving like the cosmos, and all our ancestors move with and take steps with us. Not only our ancestors, but our children and their children move with us. The one contains the all. When we're capable of making a peaceful, happy step, all our ancestors are making the step at the same time.

We know that our parents, our ancestors, and our teachers

all expect us to live our lives in a way that will protect our planet. We have to allow our ancestors, our teachers, and the Buddha in us to act. We should maintain an ongoing conversation with our ancestors, both spiritual and genetic, so that we can continually renew our insight and determination on the path of service, love, and protection. Our time, our life, is for fulfilling the expectations that our spiritual and blood ancestors and our teachers have of us. We should not allow time to slip away without realizing that living and practising this way will bring us a lot of joy and will allow us to transmit the best things we have received from our ancestors to our children and their children.

7

CARING FOR THE ENVIRONMENTALIST

A student asked me, 'There are so many urgent problems, what should I do?' I said, 'Take one thing and do it very deeply and carefully, and you will be doing everything at the same time.'

~

Many people are aware of the Earth's suffering, and their hearts are filled with compassion. They know what needs to be done, and they engage in political, social, and environmental work to try to change things. But after a period of intense involvement, they often become discouraged because they lack the strength needed to sustain a life of action. Intellect alone is not enough to guide a life of compassionate action. To effectively influence the future of our world we need something more. Real strength can be found not in power, money, or weapons, but in deep, inner peace. When we have enough insight, we are not caught by many difficult situations any more. We can get out of difficult situations very easily. When we change our daily lives—the way we think, speak, and act—we change the world. It is important for us to live in such a way that in every moment we are deeply there with our true presence, always alive and nourishing the insight of interbeing. Without peace and happiness we cannot take care of ourselves, other species, or the planet. That's why the best way to care for the environment is to care for the environmentalist.

There are many Buddhist teachings that can help us understand our interconnectedness with our Mother Earth. One of the deepest is the Diamond Sutra, which is written in the form of a dialogue between the Buddha and one of his important disciples, Subhuti. The Diamond Sutra is the most ancient text on deep ecology. It begins with this question by Subhuti: 'If daughters and sons of good families wish to give rise to the highest, most fulfilled, awakened mind, what should they rely on and what should they do to master their thinking?'

This is the same as asking, 'If I want to use my whole being to protect life, what methods and principles should I use?'

The Buddha answers, 'We have to do our best to help every living being cross the ocean of suffering. But after all beings have arrived at the shore of liberation, no being at all has been carried to the other shore. If you are still caught in the idea of a self, a person, a living being, or a life span, you are not an authentic bodhisattva.'

Self, person, living being, and life span are four notions that prevent us from seeing reality.

Life is one; we don't need to slice it into pieces and call this or that piece a 'self'. What we call a self is made only of non-self elements. When we look at a flower, for example, we may think that it is different from things that are 'non-flowers'. But when we look more deeply, we see that everything in the cosmos is in that flower. Without all of the non-flower elements—sunshine, clouds, earth, gardener, minerals, heat, rivers, and consciousness—a flower cannot be. That is why the Buddha teaches that the self does not exist. We have to discard all distinctions between self and non-self. How can anyone work to protect the environment without this insight?

The second notion the Diamond Sutra advises us to throw away is the notion of a person, a human being. This is not too difficult. When we look into the human being, we see human ancestors, animal ancestors, plant ancestors, and mineral ancestors. We see that the human is made of non-human elements. We usually discriminate between humans and non-humans, thinking that we are more important than other species. But since we humans are made of non-human elements, to protect ourselves we have to protect all of the non-human elements. There is no other way. If you think that God created humans in His own image and that He created all the other things for humans to use, then you are already discriminating and making people more important than other beings. When we see that humans have no self, we see that to take care of the environment (the non-human elements) is to take care of humanity. We have to respect and protect other species in order for us to have a chance. The best way to take good care of human beings so that they can be truly healthy and happy is to take care of other beings and the environment.

I know ecologists who are not happy in their families. They work hard to improve the environment, partly to escape their own unhappy family lives. If someone is not happy within herself, how can she help the environment? To protect the non-human elements is to protect humans, and to protect humans is to protect non-human elements.

The third notion we have to break through is the notion of a living being. We think that we living beings are different from inanimate objects, but according to the principle of interbeing, living beings are comprised of non-living being elements. When we look into ourselves, we see minerals and all other non-living being elements. Why discriminate against what we call inanimate? To protect living beings, we must protect the stones, the soil, and the oceans. Before the atomic bomb was dropped on Hiroshima, there were many beautiful stone benches in the parks. When the Japanese were rebuilding their city, they felt that these stones were dead. So they carried them away and buried them, and brought in live stones. Don't think these things are not alive. Atoms are always moving. Electrons move at nearly the speed of light. According to the teachings of Buddhism, atoms and stones are consciousness itself. That is why discrimination by living beings against non-living beings should be discarded.

The last notion is that of life span. We think that we have been alive since a certain point in time and that prior to that moment, our life did not exist. This distinction between life and non-life is not correct. Life is made of death, and death is made of life. We have to accept death; it makes life possible. The cells in our bodies are dying every day, but we never think to organize a funeral for them. The death of one cell allows the birth of another. Life and death are two aspects of the same reality. We must learn to die peacefully so that others may live. This deep meditation brings forth non-fear, non-anger, and non-despair, the strengths we need for our work. With non-fear, even when we see that a problem is huge, we won't burn out. We'll know how to make small, steady steps.

If those who work to protect the environment look deeply into these four notions, they will know how to be and how to act. They'll have enough energy and insight to be a bodhisattva on the path of action.

There's a lot of suffering in the world, and it's important for us to stay in touch with this suffering in order to be compassionate. But to remain strong, we also need to embrace the positive elements. When we see a group of people living mindfully, smiling and behaving in a loving manner, we gain confidence in our future. When we practise mindful breathing, smiling, resting, walking, and working, we become a positive element in society, and we will inspire confidence in everyone around us. This is the way to avoid allowing despair to overwhelm us. It is also the way to help the younger generation so they don't lose hope. It's very important that we live our daily lives in such a way as to demonstrate that a future is possible.

To bring about real change in our global ecological

situation our efforts must be collective and harmonious, based on love and respect for ourselves and each other, our ancestors, and future generations. If anger at injustice is what we use as the source of our energy, we may do something harmful, something we will later regret. According to Buddhism, compassion is the only source of energy that is useful and safe. With compassion your energy is born from insight; it's not blind energy. Just feeling compassion is not enough; we have to learn to express it. That is why love must always go together with understanding. Understanding and insight show us how to act.

The term 'engaged Buddhism' was created to restore the true meaning of Buddhism. Engaged Buddhism is simply Buddhism applied in our daily lives. If it's not engaged, it can't be called Buddhism. Buddhist practice takes place not only in monasteries, meditation halls, and Buddhist institutes, but in whatever situation we find ourselves. Engaged Buddhism means the activities of daily life combined with the practice of mindfulness.

There is a real need to bring Buddhism into the life of society, especially when you find yourself in a situation of war or social injustice. During the Vietnam War it became very clear that we should make Buddhism engaged, so that compassion and understanding could become part of people's daily lives. When your village is bombed and destroyed and when your neighbours become refugees, you can't continue to simply practise sitting meditation in the meditation hall. Even if your temple hasn't been bombed and your meditation hall is intact, you can still hear the cries of wounded children and you can see the pain of adults whose homes have been destroyed. How can you continue to sit there in the early morning, in the evening, and at noontime? That is why you have to find ways to bring your practice into daily life and go out to help people. You can do all you can to relieve their suffering. Yet you also know that if you abandon your practice of sitting, of walking in mindfulness, that you will not be able to continue for a long time.

It's important that while volunteering or taking part in environmental activism, we find ways to continue with our practice of mindful breathing, mindful walking, and mindful speaking. Let us not give in to anger or despair when reflecting on the current state of the world or when confronted with those who engage in the wasteful use of resources. Instead we can make our own lives an example of simple living. Deep listening and loving speech can help support the transformation of individuals and society and nurture the collective awakening that will save our civilization and our planet.

If we want to be successful in the practice of loving speech, we need to know how to manage and deal with our emotions when they surface. Every time anger, frustration, or sadness surfaces, we have to have the capacity to deal with it. This doesn't mean we fight with it, suppress it, or chase it away. Our anger and disappointment is part of us, and we should not fight against it or suppress it. When we oppress ourselves, we commit violence against ourselves. If we know how to return to our mindful breathing, we bring about our true presence and generate the energy of being in touch. With that energy we can recognize and embrace our sadness, anger, or disappointment with loving kindness.

Social work and relief work done without mindfulness practice cannot be described as engaged Buddhism. People who do this work can lose themselves in despair, anger, or disappointment. If you're really practising engaged Buddhism, then you know how to preserve yourself as a practitioner while you do things to help the people in the world. Truly engaged Buddhism is first of all practising mindfulness in all that we do.

The practice of mindfulness helps us to be aware of what is going on. Once we are able to see deeply into the suffering and recognize its roots, we will be motivated to act and to practise. The energy we need is not fear or anger, but the energy of understanding and compassion. There is no need to blame or condemn. Those who are destroying themselves, societies, and the planet aren't doing it intentionally. Their pain and loneliness are overwhelming and they want to escape. They need to be helped, not punished. Only understanding and compassion on a collective level can liberate us.

8

THE CITY WITH ONLY ONE TREE

~

Imagine a city that has only one tree left. The people who live in this city are mentally ill because they have become so alienated from nature. Finally, a doctor who lives in the city realizes why people are getting sick, and he offers each of his patients this prescription: 'You are sick because you are cut off from Mother Nature. Every morning, take a bus, go to the tree in the center of the city, and hug it for fifteen minutes. Look at the beautiful green tree and smell its fragrant bark.'

After three months of practising this, the patients feel much better. But because so many people suffer from the same malady and the doctor always gives the same prescription, after a short time, the line of people waiting their turn to embrace the tree gets to be very long, more than a mile, and people begin to get impatient. Fifteen minutes is now too long for each person to hug the tree, so the City Council legislates a five-minute maximum. Then they have to shorten it to one minute, and then only a few seconds. Finally, there is no remedy for all the sickness.

If we're not mindful, we may soon be in that situation. We have to remember that our bodies are not limited to what lies within the boundaries of our skin. Our bodies are much more immense. We know that if our heart stops beating, the flow of our life will stop, but we don't take the time to notice the many things outside of our bodies that are equally essential for our survival. If the ozone layer around the Earth were to disappear for even an instant, we would die. If the sun were to stop shining, the flow of life would stop.

Suppose in sitting meditation, I focus my attention on my heart:

Breathing in, I am aware of my heart.
Breathing out, I smile to my heart.

I may realize that the heart inside my body is not my only heart—I have many other hearts. The sun in the sky is also my heart. If my own heart failed I would die instantly. But if the other heart, the sun, explodes or stops functioning, I will also die right away. The sun is our second heart, our heart outside of our body. It gives all life on Earth the warmth necessary for existence. Plants live, thanks to the sun. Their leaves absorb the sun's energy, along with carbon dioxide from the air, to produce food for the tree, the flowers, the plankton. And thanks to the plants, we and other animals can live. All of us—people, animals, plants, and minerals—'consume' the sun, directly and indirectly. We cannot begin to describe all the effects of the sun, that great heart outside our body. When we see things in this way, we can easily transcend the duality of self and non-self. We see that we must take care of our environment because the environment is us.

When we look at green vegetables, we should know that it's not only the vegetables that are green, but the sun is also green. The green colour of the leaves is due to the presence of the sun. Without the sun, no living being could survive. Without sun, water, air, and soil, there would be no vegetables. The vegetables are the coming together of many conditions near and far.

There is no phenomenon in the universe that does not intimately concern us, from a pebble resting at the bottom of the ocean to the movement of a galaxy millions of light years away. All phenomena are interdependent. When we think of a speck of dust, a flower, or a human being, our thinking cannot break loose from the idea of a self, of a solid, permanent thing. We see a line drawn between one and many, this and that. When we truly realize the interdependent nature of the dust, the flower, and the human being, we see that unity cannot exist without diversity. Unity and diversity interpenetrate each other freely. Unity is diversity, and diversity is unity. This is the principle of interbeing.

If you are a mountain climber or someone who enjoys the countryside and the forest, you know that the trees are our lungs outside of our bodies. Yet we've acted in a way that's resulted in millions of square miles of land being deforested, and we've also destroyed the air, the rivers, and parts of the ozone layer. We're imprisoned in our small selves, thinking only of having some comfortable conditions for this small self, while we destroy our large self. If we want to change the situation, we must begin by being our true selves. To be our true selves means we have to be the forest, the river, and the ozone layer.

If we visualize ourselves as the forest, we will experience the hopes and fears of the trees. If we aren't able to do this, the forests will die, and we lose our chance for peace. When we understand that we inter-are with the trees, we will know that it's up to us to make an effort to keep the trees alive. In the last several decades, our automobiles and factories have created acid rain that has destroyed many trees. Because we inter-are with the trees, we know that if they aren't able to live, we too will disappear very soon. If the Earth were your body, you would be able to feel many areas where she is suffering.

We are all children of the Earth, and, at some time, she will take us back to herself again. We are continually arising from Mother Earth, being nurtured by her, and then returning to her.

All life is impermanent. Like us, plants are born, live for a period of time, and then return to the Earth. When they decompose, they fertilize our gardens. Living vegetables and decomposing vegetables are part of the same reality. Without one, the other cannot be. After six months, compost becomes fresh vegetables again. Plants and the Earth rely on each other. Whether the Earth is fresh, beautiful, and green, or arid and parched depends on the plants. It also depends on us.

So many beings in the universe love us unconditionally. A bird's song can express joy, beauty, and purity, and evoke in us vitality and love. The trees, the water, and the air don't ask anything of us; they just love us. Even though we need this kind of love, we continue to destroy these things. We should try our best to do the least harm to all living creatures. When we garden, for example, we can learn how to grow certain plants next to our vegetables and flowers that will ward off harmful insects, deer, and rabbits without hurting them. We can use organic repellents instead of chemical pesticides in order to protect birds and honeybees. We can always strive to reduce the harm we cause to other creatures. By destroying the animals, the air, and the trees, we are destroying ourselves. We must learn to practice unconditional love for all beings so that the animals, the air, the trees, and the minerals can continue to be themselves.

An oak tree is an oak tree. All it needs to do is to be itself. If an oak tree is less than an oak tree, we will all be in trouble. In our former lives we were rocks, clouds, and trees. We have also been an oak tree. This is not just Buddhist; it is scientific. We humans are a young species. We were plants, we were trees, and now we have become humans. We have to remember our past existences and be humble. We can learn a lot from an oak tree.

Our ecology should be a deep ecology and not only deep, but universal. There is pollution in our consciousness. Television, movies, and magazines can be ways of learning or they can be forms of pollution. They can sow seeds of violence and anxiety in us and pollute our consciousness. These things destroy us in the same way that we destroy our environment by farming with chemicals, clear-cutting trees, and polluting the water. We need to protect the ecological integrity of the Earth and an ecology of the mind, or this kind of violence and recklessness will spill over into even more areas of life.

We humans think we're intelligent, but an orchid, for example, knows how to produce symmetrical flowers; a snail knows how to make a beautiful, well-proportioned shell. Compared with their knowledge, ours is not worth much at all. We should bow deeply before the orchid and the snail and join our palms reverently before the butterfly and the magnolia tree. The feeling of respect for all species will help us to recognize and cultivate the noblest nature in ourselves.

9

TRANSFORMING OUR COMMUNITIES

Aware of the suffering and degradation brought about by the unsustainable use of material resources on the Earth, we are determined to find ways to use resources with mindfulness and with a clear view to the long-term effects of their use on future generations and ourselves. Knowing that collective suffering such as global climate change, deforestation, water scarcity, and the pollution of the air, soil, and water arises from the daily actions of human beings, we are committed to transforming our way of life in order to bring about peace and harmony within our family, our local communities and ecosystems, and the world.

—Deer Park Ecological Initiative

~

In our own monasteries and practice centers in Europe and North America, we have adopted a number of ecological initiatives to protect the climate and help people become aware of what they can do to lessen their impact on the Earth. In December 2007, our Deer Park Monastery in Escondido, California, went 100 per cent solar. All our electricity is now created by the clean energy of the sun.* Our groundbreaking ceremony was very moving. More than 1,000 practitioners attended and many of us had tears of joy in our eyes. By converting to solar energy we are lightening our steps on the Earth, so we can truly arrive as responsible and loving children of the Earth.

Our Sangha aspires to live in harmony with the land, with all the vegetation and animals, and with all our brothers and sisters. When we are in harmony with each other, we are also in harmony with the land. We see our close relationship with every person and every species. The happiness and suffering of all humans and all other species is our own happiness and suffering. We inter-are. As practitioners we see that we are part of and not separate from the whole of human civilization. As human beings we see that we are children of the Earth and not separate from the soil, the forests, the rivers, and the sky. We share the same destiny.

Much harm has been done to the Earth out of our ignorance, craving, and arrogance. As children of this land we are determined to begin anew—to make all efforts, large and

*Deer Park's 66-kilowatt photovoltaic system generates all the monastery's electricity needs and prevents 120 tons of carbon emissions from being released into the atmosphere every year.

small, to collectively effect real change in our global ecological situation. Our community made a vow not to deplete the energy of the land and her resources with our careless actions, but rather to contribute to the regeneration of this beautiful land, bringing freshness, peace, and happiness to all who come here. We have begun to use fewer cars, and to use instead electric cars and cars that run on recycled vegetable oil, which can reduce by half the emissions of carbon dioxide (CO2) gases released. We do our community shopping only once a week. We have planted native plants to reduce water use, we compost and recycle, and we have replaced all lighting with energy-efficient light bulbs.

We are also practising a No-Car Day once a week to reduce our gas consumption. One day a week is not enough, but it is something—something that demonstrates our awakening, our willingness to act, to practise mindfulness of consumption. Adopting the practice of No-Car Days has given us a lot of joy because we know that we're doing something. We don't want to be victims of despair. Our message is first and foremost a non-verbal one; our message is our own action.

As we reduce our driving and help ourselves, the planet, and the Buddha in all of us to breathe more easily, we see that even a very small choice like not using the car in the monastery compound can make good things happen. When you come to Deer Park and park your car down in the main parking lot and use your feet to walk to the upper part of the monastery grounds, you are giving yourself an opportunity to experience much joy. You have a chance to practise walking meditation; from the parking lot to the meditation hall you enjoy every step.

You begin to breathe in and out mindfully and with every step you enter the Kingdom of God. And it is a real kingdom, a real Pure Land. By not using your car you keep the air clean, you have more enjoyment, and you get in touch with the trees, the flowers, the stones, the rabbits. Being in touch with the wonders of life, the sunshine, the rain, and the flowers can bring you much joy.

One morning there were several hundred of us walking leisurely, quietly, peacefully, enjoying each other, enjoying every step. We didn't talk, we weren't listening to television, radio, or even a Dharma talk. We just enjoyed walking together, in brotherhood and sisterhood, not thinking about anything, not saying anything, enjoying our in-breath, our out-breath, and our steps, touching our father, touching our mother, smiling to them. That is the Kingdom of God. Why do we deprive ourselves of that kind of wonder? Every moment like that is healing, transforming, and nourishing. We have the capacity to do that individually and also collectively as a community.

On the 2550th anniversary of the Buddha's birth, I proposed the idea of global No-Car Days—days when we can all celebrate together, educate people about global warming, and produce the effect of a collective awakening.* All of us can call for the practise of No-Car Days in our respective communities—if not every week, then every month—so we can draw people's attention to the dangerous situation our planet is in.** A No-Car Day is your gift to the planet. You might ride your bicycle or

---

*In an address to the United Nations Educational, Scientific, and Cultural Organization (UNESCO) on 7 October 2006, Thich Nhat Hanh recommended concrete steps to end global warming and proposed the observation of global No-Car Days.

**22 September is World Car-Free Day. Visit www.car-free-days.org to learn more about the Car-Free Days Campaign and to take the pledge.

take public transportation, or you might work at home. This must be not only a call to action, but action itself. Let us do this now, together, to wake people up before it's too late. We have to embody the message we want to send to the world. We are so busy in our daily lives that we need the Buddha every week, every day, to remind us to live in such a way that a future will be possible for our children and their children. Leaving behind a deeply wounded planet would not be very kind to our children.

Every person, every family, every community, and every country can do something to help stop the progression of global warming. Schoolteachers can talk to their students—children and young people in particular are capable of understanding difficulty and suffering, and they are fully aware of how much danger the Earth is in. Children have good ideas and the wish to share them. Sometimes the younger members of a family or a community have ways of looking at a situation that are more insightful than the point of view of their elders. When young people are able to express their ideas, they feel that they are contributing to the community. As a result, they don't feel pulled along by the current or pushed out to the margins of life. It's important for parents and teachers to listen deeply to the younger generation and encourage them to speak out.

Children are skilful at practising mindfulness and reminding others to do the same. I know many young people who know how to practise and transform their lives, and who are able to help their parents and others to transform. These children should give us great faith in our future. We're not at a dead end. We have an escape route. We just need to hold each other's hands and walk together on the path. Our ancestors also walked on that path. That path is the path of brotherhood and sisterhood, and it is more precious than any ideology or religion.

Many members of our global family are already walking together on the path. Denmark has been able to use wind energy to obtain twenty per cent of its electricity. In Iceland, ninety-three per cent of the homes are heated geothermally. The South Korean people have replanted forests. Sweden has announced the goal of having an oil-free economy. Australia has committed $500 million—more than any other government—to fighting climate change. The European Union has made climate stabilization a top priority. These are wonderful things.

Another thing we can do is to write to our political representatives and tell them what we want. When the people have a clear vision, and the people have made up their minds, then the government has no choice but to follow. Let your elected officials know you want policies funding the development of clean, renewable energy sources, and the halting of the destruction of forests. You have to support your congresspeople and your government by providing them with your insights and ideas. Individual insights help bring about collective insight, and with collective insight there will be group action. We have to become the government's supporters and advisors. We have to tell them that the defence budget worldwide is out of sync with everything else. One-sixth of that budget could make a change that would save the planet. The United Nations Security Council should work on that. It's urgent. Ask the nations of the world to use one-sixth of their military budget to save our Earth. This is reasonable, and it is possible.

Acts like organizing No-Car Days can free us from our everyday preoccupations so that we are able to see that there is violence invading the world. If you really want to continue the career of the Buddha, you have to help this collective awakening. It's important to have the support of your family or community. When we live in a community where everyone practises mindful consumption, it's easy for us to practise mindful consumption. We will do this as a Sangha, with brotherhood and sisterhood, and in this way no single person has to worry.

10

THE EYES OF THE ELEPHANT QUEEN

Every step we make has the power to heal and transform. Not only can we heal ourselves by our steps, but we can help heal the Earth and the environment.

~

The Mahaparinirvana Sutra describes the life of the Buddha during his last year—the places he travelled, the people he met, and the teachings he gave. In the sutra, it is said that the Buddha had just spent the Rains Retreat near the city of Vaishali, north of the Ganges river, and that he then decided to travel north in order to return to the town of his birth, Kapilavastu. Although he knew this was the last time he would ever see the beautiful city of Vaishali, he did not lift his hand to wave goodbye. Instead, we find this sentence in the sutra:

The Buddha, on his way, turned around; and with the eyes of an elephant queen, he surveyed the city of Vaishali for the last time and said, 'Ananda, don't you think that Vaishali is beautiful?'

After having surveyed the city of Vaishali with a gentle gaze that took in all of its beauty, the Buddha turned back to the north and began to walk.

When the Buddha looks, he does so with the eyes of the elephant queen in order to look deeply and recognize what is there. We, too, have the eyes of the Buddha and of the elephant queen. If you see deeply into the beauty of nature around you, you're looking with the eyes of the Buddha. It is extremely kind of you to look on behalf of the Buddha, to contemplate the world for the Buddha, because you are his continuation.

So when you practise sitting meditation, sit for the Buddha. The Buddha in you is sitting upright, the Buddha in you is enjoying every in-breath and out-breath, the Buddha in you is contemplating the world with mindfulness and getting in touch with the beauty of nature.

If you know how to contemplate the beauty of nature with the eyes of the Buddha, you will not say that your life has no meaning. You can listen with the ears of the Buddha, you can contemplate the world with the eyes of the Buddha, and thanks to that, your children and their children will also be able to look and contemplate like the Buddha. You transmit the Buddha to your children and to their children, in the way you walk, sit, look, and listen, even in the way you eat. This is something that you can do now. Starting today, you can already be a real and true continuation of the Buddha, our spiritual ancestor.

Every minute of our daily lives is an opportunity for us to walk like a buddha, to listen with compassion like a buddha, to sit as peacefully and as happily as a buddha, and to look deeply and enjoy the beauties of the world like a buddha. In doing so, we are helping our father, our mother, our ancestors, and our children in us to evolve, and we are also helping our teacher to fulfil his vow, his aspiration. In this way, our life will truly become a concrete message of love. Living out lives in this way, we can help prevent global warming from harming our planet.

When we look deeply into ourselves, we can identify elements of the Kingdom of God that are available in the here and now. To me the Kingdom of God or the Pure Land of the Buddha is not a vague idea; it is a reality. That pine tree standing on the mountain is so beautiful, solid, and green. To me the pine tree belongs to the Kingdom of God, the Pure Land of the Buddha. Your beautiful child with her fresh smile belongs to the Kingdom of God, and you also belong to the Kingdom of God. If we're capable of recognizing the flowing river, the blue sky, the blossoming tree, the singing bird, the majestic mountains, the countless animals, the sunlight, the fog, the snow, the innumerable wonders of life as miracles that belong to the Kingdom of God, we'll do our best to preserve them and not allow them to be destroyed. If we recognize that this planet belongs to the Kingdom of God, we will cherish and protect it so we can enjoy it for a long time, and so that our children and their children will have a chance to enjoy it.

The Buddha teaches us about the cycle of *samsara,* a cycle in which the same suffering repeats itself. If we don't practise, we won't be able to step out of it. With mindful breathing, mindful walking, and mindful dwelling in the present moment, we don't need to consume and run after objects of craving in order to be happy. In our monastery at Plum Village, nobody has their own bank account, no one has a private car or a private cell phone, and the monks, nuns, and laypeople who live here don't receive any salary. And yet there's joy and happiness, there's brotherhood and sisterhood. We don't need the 'American dream' any more. Breathing in, we get in touch with the stars, the moon, the clouds, the mountain, the river. When we're inhabited by the energy of mindfulness and concentration, every step we take leads us into the Kingdom of God, the Pure Land of the Buddha.

When we look deeply into a flower, we see the elements that have come together to allow it to manifest. We can see clouds manifesting as rain. Without the rain, nothing can grow. When I touch the flower, I'm touching the cloud and touching the ram. This is not just poetry, it's reality. If we take the clouds and the rain out of the flower, the flower will not be there. With the eye of the Buddha, we are able to see the clouds and the rain in the flower. We can touch the sun without burning our fingers. Without the sun nothing can grow, so it's not possible to take the sun out of the flower. The flower cannot be as a separate entity; it has to inter-be with the light, with the clouds, with the rain. The word 'interbeing' is closer to reality than the word 'being'. *Being* really means *interbeing*.

The same is true for me, for you, and for the Buddha. The Buddha has to inter-be with everything. Interbeing and non-self are the objects of our contemplation. We have to train ourselves so that in our daily lives we can touch the truth of interbeing and non-self in every moment. You are in touch with the clouds, with the rain, with the children, with the trees, with the rivers, with your planet, and that contact reveals the true nature of reality, the nature of impermanence, non-self, interdependence, and interbeing.

We have destroyed our Mother Earth in the same way bacteria or a virus can destroy a human body. Mother Earth is also a body. Of course, there are bacteria that are beneficial to the human body, that protect the body and help generate enzymes that we need. Similarly, if the human species wakes up and knows how to live with responsibility, compassion, and loving kindness, the human species can be a living organism with the capacity to protect the body of Mother Earth. We have to see that we inter-are with our Mother Earth, that we live with her and die with her.

It's wonderful to realize that we are all in a family, we are all children of the Earth. We should take care of each other and we should take care of our environment, and this is possible with the practice of being together as a large family. A positive change in individual awareness will bring about a positive change in the collective awareness. Protecting the planet must be given the first priority. I hope you will take the time to sit down with each other, have tea with your friends and your family, and discuss these things. Invite Bodhisattva Earth Holder to sit and collaborate with you. Then make your decision and act to save our beautiful planet. Changing your way of living will bring you a lot of joy right away and, with your first mindful breath, healing will begin.

PART THREE

PRACTICES FOR MINDFUL LIVING

EARTH GATHAS: MEDITATIONS FOR DAILY LIFE

Gathas help us to practise mindfulness in our daily lives and to look deeply. Reciting these short verses will bring awareness, peace, and joy to the simple activities we may take for granted, like eating a meal, washing our hands, taking out the garbage. The images are all real and practical. You might even try to create your own gathas for the things that are important to you: riding your bicycle, putting on a warm scarf, taking your dog for a walk. Gathas remind us that the Earth provides us with precious gifts every day.

TAKING THE FIRST STEP OF THE DAY

Walking on the Earth
is a miracle!
Each mindful step
reveals the wondrous Dharmakaya.

This poem can be recited right as we get out of bed and our feet touch the floor. It can also be used during walking meditation or any time we stand up and walk. Dharmakaya literally means the 'body' (kaya) of the Buddha's teachings (Dharma), the way of understanding and love. Before passing away, the Buddha told his disciples, 'Only my physical body will pass away. My Dharma body will remain with you forever.' Dharmakaya also means the essence of all that exists. All phenomena—the song of a bird, the warm rays of the sun, a cup of hot tea—are manifestations of the Dharmakaya. We, too, are of the same nature as these wonders of the universe. We do not have to walk in space or on water to experience a miracle; the real miracle is to be awake in the present moment. Walking on the green Earth, we realize the wonder of being alive. When we make steps like this, the sun of the Dharmakaya will shine.

TURNING ON THE WATER

Water flows from high mountain sources.
Water runs deep in the Earth.
Miraculously, water comes to us
and sustains all life.

Even if we know the source of our water, we often take its appearance for granted. But water is what makes all life on Earth possible. Our bodies are more than seventy per cent water. Because of water, fruits and vegetables grow and we have enough food to eat. Water is a good friend, a bodhisattva, which nourishes the many thousands of species on Earth. Its benefits are infinite. Reciting this gatha before turning on the faucet or drinking a glass of water enables us to see the stream of fresh water in our own hearts so that we feel completely refreshed. To celebrate the gift of water is to cultivate awareness and help sustain our life and the lives of others.

WASHING YOUR HANDS

Water flows over these hands.
May I use them skilfully
to preserve our precious planet.

Our beautiful Earth is endangered. We are exhausting her resources and polluting her rivers, lakes, and oceans, destroying the habitats of many species, including our own. We are destroying the forests, the soil, the air, and the ozone layer. Because of our ignorance and fears, our planet may be destroyed as an environment that is hospitable to human life. The Earth stores water, and water gives life. Observe your hands as the water runs over them. Do you have enough clear insight to preserve and protect this beautiful planet, our Mother Earth?

LOOKING AT YOUR EMPTY BOWL

My bowl, empty now,
will soon be filled with precious food.
Beings all over the Earth are struggling to live.
How fortunate I am to have enough to eat.

When many people on this Earth look at an empty bowl, they know their bowl will continue to be empty for a long time. So the empty bowl is as important to honour as the full bowl. We are grateful to have food to eat, and with this gatha, we can vow to find ways to help those who are hungry.

SERVING FOOD

In this food,
I see clearly
the entire universe
supporting my existence.

When we look at our plate, filled with fragrant and appetizing food, we should be aware of the bitter pain of people who suffer from hunger and malnutrition. Looking at our plate, we can see Mother Earth, the farm workers, and the tragedy of the unequal distribution of resources. We who live in North America and Europe are accustomed to eating foods imported from other countries, whether it is coffee from Colombia, chocolate from Ghana, or fragrant rice from Thailand. Many children in these countries, except those from rich families, never see the fine products that are put aside for export in order to bring in money. Before a meal, we can join our palms in mindfulness and think about those who do not have enough to eat. Slowly and mindfully, we breathe three times and recite this gatha. Doing so will help us maintain mindfulness. May we find ways to live more simply in order to have more time and energy to change the system of injustice that exists in the world.

TOUCHING THE EARTH

Earth brings us into life and nourishes us.
Earth takes us back again.
We are born and we die with every breath.

The Earth is our mother. All life arises from her and is nourished by her. Each of us is a child of the Earth and, at some time, the Earth will take us back to her again. In fact, we are continuously coming to life and returning to the bosom of the Earth. We who practise meditation should be able to see birth and death in every breath. Touching the Earth, letting your fingers feel the soil, and gardening are wonderful, restorative activities. If you live in a city, you may not have many opportunities to hoe the soil, plant vegetables, or take care of flowers.... But you can still find and appreciate a small patch of grass or Earth and care for it. Being in touch with Mother Earth is a wonderful way to preserve your mental health.

WATERING THE GARDEN

Water and sun
green these plants.
When the rain of compassion falls,
even the desert becomes a vast fertile plain.

Water is the balm of compassion. It has the capacity to restore us to life. Rain enlivens crops and protects people from hunger. The Bodhisattva of Compassion is often depicted holding a vase of water in her left hand, and a willow branch in her right. She sprinkles down compassion, like drops of nurturing water, to revitalize tired hearts and minds weak from suffering. Watering the garden, the compassionate rain falls on the plants. When we offer water to plants, we offer it to the whole Earth. When watering plants, if we speak to them, we are also speaking to ourselves. We exist in relationship to all other phenomena. The feeling of alienation among so many people today has come about because they lack awareness of the interconnectedness of all things. We cannot separate ourselves from society or anything else. *This is like this, because that is like that* is a phrase taken from the sutras, summarizing the principle of interrelatedness. To water plants and experience compassion and interconnectedness is a wonderful practice of meditation.

RECYCLING

In the garbage, I see a rose.
In the rose, I see the garbage.
Everything is in transformation.
Even permanence is impermanent.

Whenever we throw something away, whether in the garbage can, the compost, or the recycling, it can smell terrible. Rotting organic matter smells especially terrible. But it can also become rich compost for fertilizing the garden. The fragrant rose and the stinking garbage are two sides of the same existence. Without one, the other cannot be. Everything is in transformation. The rose that wilts after six days will become a part of the garbage. After six months the garbage is transformed into a rose. When we speak of impermanence, we understand that everything is in transformation. This becomes that, and that becomes this. Looking deeply, we can contemplate one thing and see everything else in it. We are not disturbed by change when we see the interconnectedness and continuity of all things. It is not that the life of any individual is permanent, but that life itself continues. When we identify ourselves with life and go beyond the boundaries of a separate identity, we shall be able to see permanence in the impermanent, or the rose in the garbage.

THE FIVE AWARENESSES BREATHING EXERCISE

Breathing in, I know I am of the nature to grow old.
Breathing out, I know I cannot escape old age.

Breathing in, I know I am of the nature to get sick.
Breathing out, I know I cannot escape sickness.

Breathing in, I know I am of the nature to die.
Breathing out, I know I cannot escape dying.

Breathing in, I know one day I will have to let go of everything and everyone I cherish.
Breathing out, there is no way to bring them along.

Breathing in, I know that I bring nothing with me except my actions, thoughts, and deeds.
Breathing out, only my actions come with me.

DEEP RELAXATION

Resting is a precondition for healing. When animals in the forest get wounded, they find a place to lie down and they rest completely for many days. They don't think about food or anything else. They just rest, and they get the healing they need. When we humans become overcome with stress, we may go to the pharmacy and get drugs. But we don't stop. We don't know how to help ourselves.

Stress accumulates in our body. The way we eat, drink, and live takes its toll on our well-being. Deep relaxation is an opportunity for our body to rest, to heal, and be restored. We relax our body, giving our attention to each part in turn, and sending our love and care to every cell.

Mindful breathing and total relaxation of the body can be done at home at least once a day. It may last for twenty minutes or longer. The living room can be used to practise total relaxation. One member of the family can lead the session of total relaxation. And the young people can learn how to lead a session of total relaxation for the whole family.

I think in the twenty-first century we have to set up a hall for total relaxation in school. If you are a school teacher, you can master the techniques and invite your students to practise it before class or halfway through the class, in a sitting position or a lying position. Teachers and students can enjoy practising mindful breathing and total relaxation together. This helps the teachers have less stress, and it helps the students and brings the spiritual dimension into the school. If you are a doctor you can master the techniques and help your patients. If your patients know the art of mindful breathing and total relaxation, their capacity to heal themselves will increase and the process of healing will take place more quickly. In the National Assembly in the Congress, the members can also practise total relaxation and mindful breathing. Sometimes the debates in the Parliament can go late into the night. Many members are under stress. We want our Parliament to be relaxed, to feel well, in order to make the best decision they can make. This is a practice that is not sectarian or religious; it's scientific. One session of practice can already bring good results to everyone who practises. It's very important to practise deep relaxation.

If you have trouble sleeping, deep relaxation can compensate. Lying awake in your bed, you may like to practise total relaxation and follow your breathing in and breathing out. Sometimes it can help you to get some sleep. But even if you don't sleep, the practise is still very good because it can nourish you and allow you to rest. You can also listen to beautiful chanting; that can help very much with releasing and nourishing. It's very important to allow yourself to rest.

When we do deep relaxation in a group, one person can guide the exercise using the following cues or some variation of them. When you do deep relaxation on your own, you may like to record an exercise to follow as you practice.

DEEP RELAXATION EXERCISE

Lie down on your back with your arms at your sides. Make yourself comfortable. Allow your body to relax. Be aware of the floor underneath you...and of the contact of your body with the floor. *(Pause)* Allow your body to sink into the floor. *(Pause)*

Become aware of your breathing, in and out. Be aware of your abdomen rising and falling as you breathe in and out *(pause)*...rising...falling...rising...falling. *(Pause)*

Breathing in, bring your awareness to your eyes. Breathing out, allow your eyes to relax. Allow your eyes to sink back into your head...let go of the tension in all the tiny muscles around your eyes...our eyes allow us to see a paradise of form and colour...allow your eyes to rest...send love and gratitude to your eyes.... *(Pause)*

Breathing in, bring your awareness to your mouth. Breathing out, allow your mouth to relax. Release the tension around your mouth...your lips are the petals of a flower...let a gentle smile bloom on your lips...smiling releases the tension in the hundreds of muscles in your face...feel the tension release in your cheeks...your jaw...your throat.... *(Pause)*

Breathing in, bring your awareness to your shoulders. Breathing out, allow your shoulders to relax. Let them sink into the floor...let all the accumulated tension flow into the floor... we carry so much on our shoulders...now let them relax as we care for our shoulders. *(Pause)*

Breathing in, become aware of your arms. Breathing out,

relax your arms. Let your arms sink into the floor...your upper arms...your elbows...your lower arms...your wrists...hands... fingers...all the tiny muscles...move your fingers a little if you need to, to help the muscles relax. *(Pause)*

Breathing in, bring your awareness to your heart. Breathing out, allow your heart to relax. *(Pause)* We have neglected our heart for a long time...by the way we work, eat, and manage anxiety and stress...*(Pause)*...our heart beats for us night and day...embrace your heart with mindfulness and tenderness... reconciling and taking care of your heart. *(Pause)*

Breathing in, bring your awareness to your legs. Breathing out, allow your legs to relax. Release all the tension in your legs...your thighs...your knees...your calves...your ankles... your feet...your toes...all the tiny muscles in your toes...you may want to move your toes a little to help them relax...send your love and care to your toes. *(Pause)*

Breathing in, breathing out...my whole body feels light... like duckweed floating on the water...I have nowhere to go... nothing to do...I am free as the cloud floating in the sky.... *(Pause)*

(Singing or music for some minutes) (Pause)

Bring your awareness back to your breathing...to your abdomen rising and falling. *(Pause)*

Following your breathing, become aware of your arms and legs...you may want to move them a little and stretch. *(Pause)*

When you feel ready, slowly sit up. *(Pause)*

When you are ready, slowly stand up.

In the above exercise you can guide awareness to any part of the body: the hair, scalp, brain, ears, neck, lungs, each of the internal organs, the digestive system, pelvis, and to any part of the body that needs healing and attention, embracing each part and sending love, gratitude, and care as we hold it in our awareness and breathe in and out.

TOUCHING THE EARTH

The practice of Touching the Earth is to return to the Earth, to our roots, to our ancestors, and to recognize that we are not alone but connected to a whole stream of spiritual and blood ancestors. We are their continuation, and with them we will continue in future generations. We touch the Earth to let go of the idea that we are separate and to remind us that we are the Earth and part of life.

When we touch the Earth we become small, with the humility and simplicity of a young child. When we touch the Earth we become great, like an ancient tree sending her roots deep into the earth, drinking from the source of all waters. When we touch the Earth, we breathe in all the strength and stability of the Earth, and breathe out our suffering—our feelings of anger, hatred, fear, inadequacy, and grief.

We join our palms to form a lotus bud and we gently lower ourselves to the ground so that all four limbs (shins and forearms) and our forehead are resting comfortably on the floor. If you prefer, you can lie down fully extended. While we are Touching the Earth we turn our palms face up, showing our openness to the Three Jewels—the Buddha, the Dharma, and the Sangha. Even after practising the Five Earth-Touchings only one or two times, we can already release a lot of our suffering and feeling of alienation and reconcile with our ancestors, parents, children, and friends.

EARTH PEACE TREATY

I

In gratitude, I bow to all generations of
ancestors in my blood family.

[BELL]
[ALL TOUCH THE EARTH]

I see my mother and father, whose blood, flesh, and vitality are circulating in my own veins and nourishing every cell in me. Through them, I see my four grandparents. Their expectations, experiences, and wisdom have been transmitted from so many generations of ancestors. I carry in me the life, blood, experience, wisdom, happiness, and sorrow of all generations. The suffering and all the elements that need to be transformed, I am practising to transform. I open my heart, flesh, and bones to receive the energy of insight, love, and experience transmitted to me by all my ancestors. I see my roots in my father, mother, grandfathers, grandmothers, and all my ancestors. I know I am only the continuation of this ancestral lineage. Please support, protect, and transmit to me your energy. I know wherever children and grandchildren are, ancestors are there, also. I know that parents always love and support their children and grandchildren, although they are not always able to express it skillfully because of difficulties they themselves encountered. I see that my ancestors tried to build a way of life based on gratitude, joy, confidence, respect, and loving kindness. As a continuation of my ancestors, I bow deeply and allow their energy to flow through me. I ask my ancestors for their support, protection, and strength.

[THREE BREATHS]

[BELL]

[ALL STAND UP]

II

In gratitude, I bow to all generations of ancestors in my spiritual family.

[BELL]

[ALL TOUCH THE EARTH]

I see in myself my teachers, the ones who show me the way of love and understanding, the way to breathe, smile, forgive, and live deeply in the present moment. I see through my teachers all teachers over many generations and traditions, going back to the ones who began my spiritual family thousands of years ago. I see the Buddha or Christ or the patriarchs and matriarchs as my teachers, and also as my spiritual ancestors. I see that their energy and that of many generations of teachers has entered me and is creating peace, joy, understanding, and loving kindness in me. I know that the energy of these teachers has deeply transformed the world. Without the Buddha and all these spiritual ancestors, I would not know the way to practise to bring peace and happiness into my life and into the lives of my family and society. I open my heart and my body to receive the energy of understanding, loving kindness, and protection from the Awakened Ones, their teachings, and the community of practise over many generations. I am their continuation. I ask these spiritual ancestors to transmit to me their infinite source of energy, peace, stability, understanding, and love. I vow to practise to transform the suffering in myself and the world, and to transmit their energy to future generations of practitioners. My spiritual ancestors may have had their own difficulties and not always been able to transmit the teachings, but I accept them as they are.

[THREE BREATHS]

[BELL]

[ALL STAND UP]

III

In gratitude, I bow to this land and all of the ancestors who made it available.

[BELL]

[ALL TOUCH THE EARTH]

I see that I am whole, protected, and nourished by this land and all of the living beings who have been here and made life easy and possible for me through all their efforts. I see Red Cloud, Harriet Tubman, Dorothy Day, Cesar Chavez, Martin Luther King, Jr, and all the others known and unknown who have struggled so that we could live better lives. I see all those who have made this country a refuge for people of so many origins and colours, by their talent, perseverance, and love—those who have worked hard to build schools, hospitals, bridges, and roads, to protect human rights, to develop science and technology, and to fight for freedom and social justice. I see myself touching my ancestors of Native American origin who have lived on this land for such a long time and have known the ways to live in peace and harmony with nature, protecting the mountains, forests, animals, vegetation, and minerals of this land. I feel the energy of this land penetrating my body and soul, supporting and accepting me. I vow to cultivate and maintain this energy and transmit it to future generations. I vow to contribute my part in transforming the violence, hatred, and delusion that still lie deep in the collective consciousness of this society so that future generations will have more safety, joy, and peace. I ask this land for its protection and support.

[THREE BREATHS]

[BELL]

[ALL STAND UP]

IV

In gratitude and compassion, I bow down and transmit my energy to those I love.

[BELL]

[ALL TOUCH THE EARTH]

All the energy I have received I now want to transmit to my father, my mother, everyone I love, all who have suffered and worried because of me and for my sake. I know I have not been mindful enough in my daily life. I also know that those who love me have had their own difficulties. They have suffered because they were not lucky enough to have an environment that encouraged their full development. I transmit my energy to my mother, my father, my brothers, my sisters, my beloved ones, my husband, my wife, my partner, my daughter, and my son, so that their pain will be relieved, so they can smile and feel the joy of being alive. I want all of them to be healthy and joyful. I know that when they are happy, I will also be happy. I no longer feel resentment towards any of them. I pray that all ancestors in my blood and spiritual families will focus their energies toward each of them, to protect and support them. I know that I am not separate from them. I am one with those I love.

[THREE BREATHS]

[BELL]

[ALL STAND UP]

V

In understanding and compassion, I bow down to reconcile myself with all those who have made me suffer.

[BELL]

[ALL TOUCH THE EARTH]

I open my heart and send forth my energy of love and understanding to everyone who has made me suffer, to those who have destroyed much of my life and the lives of those I love. I know now that these people have themselves undergone a lot of suffering and that their hearts are overloaded with pain, anger, and hatred. I know that anyone who suffers that much will make those around them suffer. I know they may have been unlucky, never having the chance to be cared for and loved. Life and society have dealt them so many hardships. They have been wronged and abused. They have not been guided in the path of mindful living. They have accumulated wrong perceptions about life, about me, and about us. They have wronged us and the people we love. I pray to my ancestors in my blood and spiritual families to channel to these persons who have made us suffer the energy of love and protection so that their hearts will be able to receive the nectar of love and blossom like a flower. I pray that they can be transformed to experience the joy of living, so that they will not continue to make themselves and others suffer. I see their suffering and do not want to hold any feelings of hatred or anger in myself toward them. I do not want them to suffer. I channel my energy of love and understanding to them and ask all my ancestors to help them.

[THREE BREATHS]

[BELL]

[ALL STAND UP]

EARTH PEACE TREATY

COMMITMENT SHEET

This sheet offers a number of steps we can take to reduce the impact of our ecological footprint. Please look over this and, if you feel inspired, commit to a few or more of them by marking the blank with a '✓' check. If you already are currently practising the step, mark an 'X' on the blank. When you are done please copy your commitments on to a piece of paper so that you can carry them with you as a reminder.

I, ______________________________________

commit to:

- Walk or bike to work _________ days per week.
- Walk or bike to places within five miles.
- Carpool to work or use mass transit.
- Reduce flight-travel to less than _________ flight-hours per year.
- Have a car-free day once a week.
- Have a car-free day once a month.
- Work at home one day a week.
- Reduce car trips by _________ per cent.
- Use stairs, not elevators.
- Have an electricity-free day once a week.
- Get an energy audit of my home and improve its efficiency.
- Purchase and install solar panels at home.
- Purchase renewable-source electricity (wind, geothermal).
- Air-dry clothes (without a dryer).
- Reduce the use of hair dryers and appliances.
- Support farmers and reduce food-miles by buying local produce.

- Grow produce at home.
- Not use pesticides or herbicides.
- Purchase __________ per cent organic food.
- Join a Community-Supported Agriculture (GSA) group near my home.
- Replace light bulbs at home with compact fluorescents.
- Eliminate the use of air-conditioning at home.
- Reduce air-conditioning at home by __________ degrees.
- Reduce heating at home by __________ degrees.
- Install a programmable thermostat at home.
- Install energy-efficient insulation and windows at home.
- Eat only vegetarian food.
- Drive a fuel-efficient vehicle.
- Avoid purchasing disposable items with lots of packaging.
- Replace paper napkins, towels, and plates with reusable equivalents.
- Use the library, instead of buying books, as much as possible.
- Use cloth or other reusable bags for shopping, etc.
- Use biodegradable cleaning products.
- Compost kitchen waste.
- Encourage office/school to recycle.
- Share magazines and catalogs by donating them to clinics, etc.
- Reuse and recycle all items possible.
- Buy clothing in used clothing/thrift shops.
- Plant native and drought-tolerant plants where applicable.
- Plant __________ trees in my neighbourhood.
- Turn off computers while not in use.
- Install a power strip for appliances to avoid drawing ghost electricity.

- Set computer and display to turn off after ten minutes of inactivity.
- Reduce use of hot water by ________ per cent.
- Take only short, warm showers.
- Install a solar water heating unit.
- Re-use gray water.
- Flush only when necessary.
- Turn off faucet while brushing teeth or shaving.
- Reduce overall water use by ________ per cent.
- Install a system to capture and store rainwater.
- Pick up trash along walking/jogging route.
- Encourage a friend to commit to items on this list.
- Educate myself on ecological issues.
- Write articles/stories to help others get in touch with their ecosystem.
- Meditate once a week on my relationship to the ecosystem in which I live.
- Meditate once a week on how I can reduce my consumption and act on this.
- Write to local and national politicians calling for more effective environmental legislation.
- Support local environmental organizations.

Add my own commitment proposals here:

Please send me an email to remind me of the commitments I have made and to receive further information about ecology projects at Deer Park Monastery.

Email: ________________________________

I make the commitment to practise the items that I have checked above so that I may reduce the ecological impact of my way of living.

Signed: ______________________________

Date: ________________________________

Mail to: Deer Park Monastery,
2499 Melru Lane, Escondido, CA 92026

Dharmacharya Shantum Seth, a teacher ordained by Thich Nhat Hanh, offers teachings and shares the practice of Mindfulness meditation in different parts of India and the world. He also leads pilgrimages, 'In the Footsteps of the Buddha'.

Please visit: www.buddhapath.com or contact info@buddhapath.com

Ahimsa Trust represents Thich Nhat Hanh and his community in India. It is a volunteer driven, non-profit trust, working to create peace, in one's self and in the world. Ahimsa Trust organizes Days of Mindfulness and retreats/workshops across India, especially for educators.

Please visit www.ahimsatrust.org or contact ahimsa.trust@gmail.com

For worldwide contacts and teachings of Thich Nhat Hanh and his community, please visit www.plumvillage.org